ALevelPhysicsOnline.com

ACKNOWLEDGEMENTS

This series of books has been a pretty big undertaking!

I'm extremely grateful to the following contributors who have helped write many of the questions in this guide. Between them, they have many years of experience as Heads of Physics, Heads or Science or Outreach Officers promoting STEM subjects.

- Dr Peter Edmunds
- Muhammad Kashif Jamal
- Dr Dan Jones
- Dave Grainger
- Matthew Lewis
- Melissa Lord

Joe Cattermole (a recent Physics Graduate) collated the first draft and wrote hundreds of additional questions before James Hills, Rufus Jones and Richard Burton assisted with formatting and proofreading the many edits that I made.

It was a real team effort and I hope the resulting book will be useful to you as you study A Level Physics.

Lewis Matheson

HOW TO USE THIS BOOK

The idea is pretty simple – attempt a few questions everyday to help build upon your existing knowledge and strengthen understanding as you commence your A Level Physics course.

To find out a little bit more about how to use this book scan the QR code, or go to the webpage below, to watch a video explaining everything you need to know.

ALevelPhysicsOnline.com/**book-2**

Please be aware that every school teaches the content in a different order. If you can not complete a question because you have not been taught that topic yet then:

- Buy Book 1 and work through this over a couple of weekends
- Do not forget what you previously learned for GCSE
- Have a look in your textbook or watch one of my videos
- Research it on the internet
- Mark thc question and come back to it at a later date
- Ask your teachers

DATA AND FORMULAE

Add useful information to this page as you're working through the book.

Resistors in Parallel

$$\frac{1}{R_T} = \frac{1}{R_1} + \frac{1}{R_2} + \ldots$$

$g = 9.81\ N\,kg^{-1}$

$m_{electron} = 9.11 \times 10^{-31}\ kg$

NOVEMBER

NOVEMBER

Welcome! Now you are firmly established in your new life as an A Level student, Book 2 will introduce you to a whole array of new topics.

Just like in Book 1, there are a few questions for you to have a go at every day. A lot of these are based on your current knowledge from GCSEs, while others are developing the topics you will cover in school. Do not worry if some of these questions are unfamiliar – you can always come back to complete these at a later date.

So, let's begin...

Worked Examples

1. Calculate the **area** of a circle with a radius of:

   a. 1.25 m $A = \pi r^2 = \pi \times 1.25^2 = 4.91\ m^2$ (3 sf)

   b. 12.5 mm $A = \pi r^2 = \pi \times (12.5 \times 10^{-3})^2 = 4.91 \times 10^{-4}\ m^2$ (3 sf)

   c. 125 μm $A = \pi r^2 = \pi \times (125 \times 10^{-6})^2 = 4.91 \times 10^{-8}\ m^2$ (Standard form)

2. Calculate the **mass** of a robin flying at 8.9 m s⁻¹ when it has a kinetic energy of 879 mJ.

   $E_k = \frac{1}{2} m v^2$ (Equation + Rearrange) $m = \frac{2E_k}{v^2} = \frac{2 \times 879 \times 10^{-3}}{8.9^2}$ (Working out; 2 sf)

   $m = 0.02219$

   $m = 2.2 \times 10^{-2}\ kg$ (2 sf; Units)

3. Calculate the **horizontal component** of a force of 9.7 N acting at 17° above the horizontal.

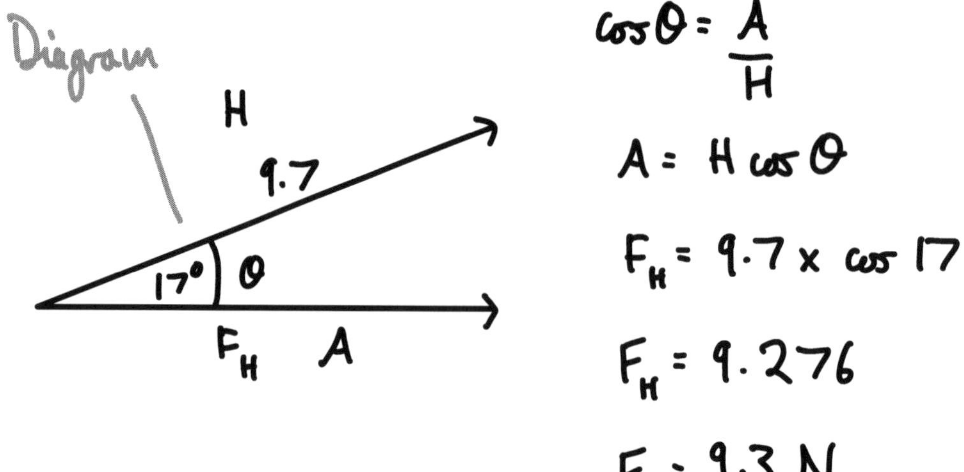

1st November

1 2 3

1. Calculate the **angle**, θ, in a triangle with a hypotenuse of length 1.2 m and an opposite side length of 1.0 m.

2. Write down the **units** for:

   a. Potential difference

   b. Resistivity

   c. Capacitance

   d. Momentum

   e. Electromotive force

   f. Magnetic flux density

3. In the circuit below are six identical 9.0 Ω resistors and a battery of e.m.f 3.0 V. Calculate the total **energy transferred per second** in this circuit.

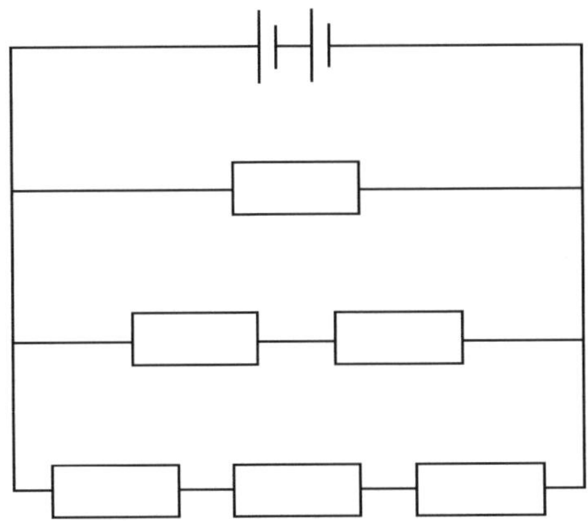

2nd November – Part 1

1. Calculate the **acceleration** at:
   a. t = 2.0 s
   b. t = 6.5 s

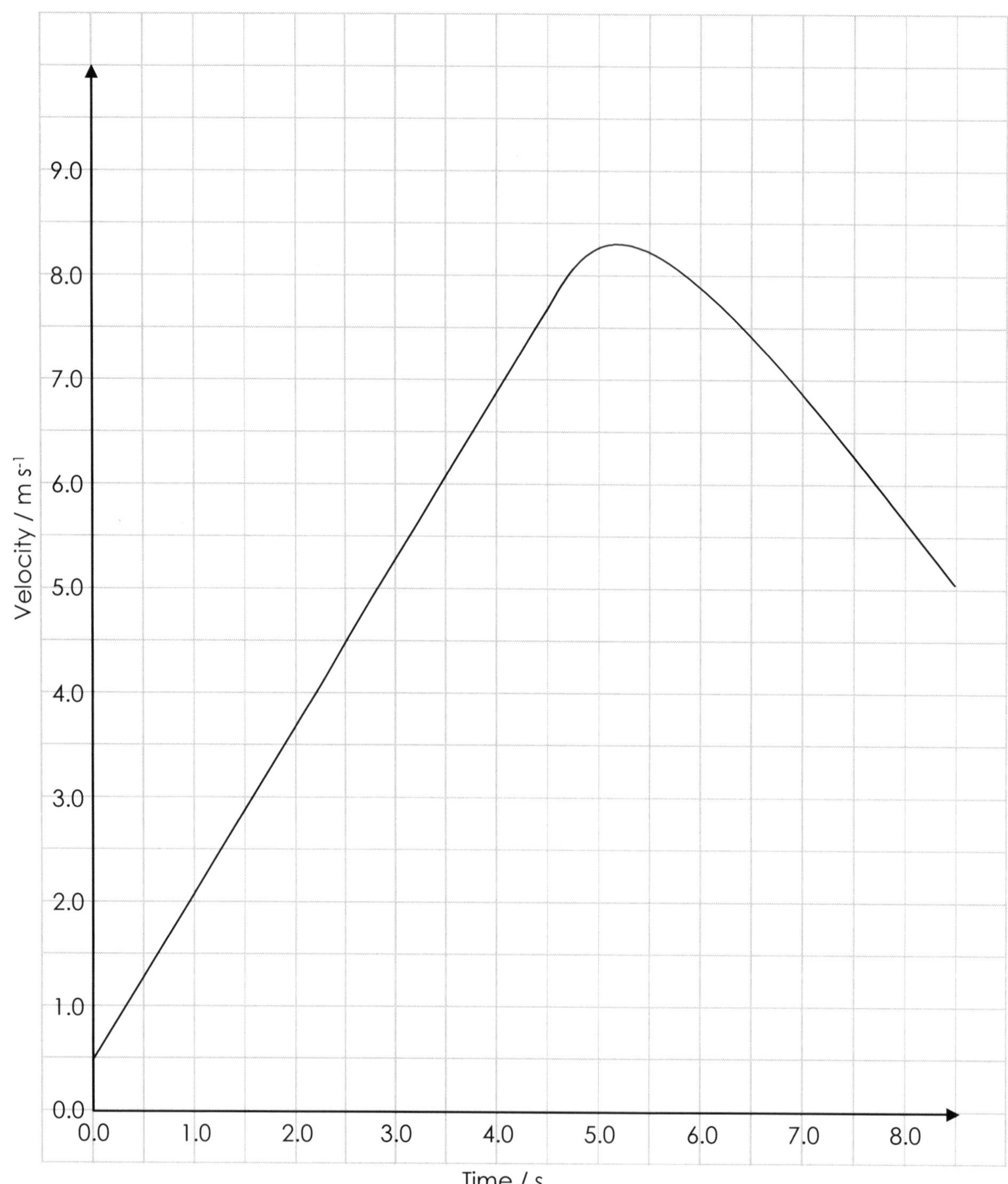

2nd November – Part 2

2. Calculate the **displacement** between t = 2.0 and t = 7.0 s.

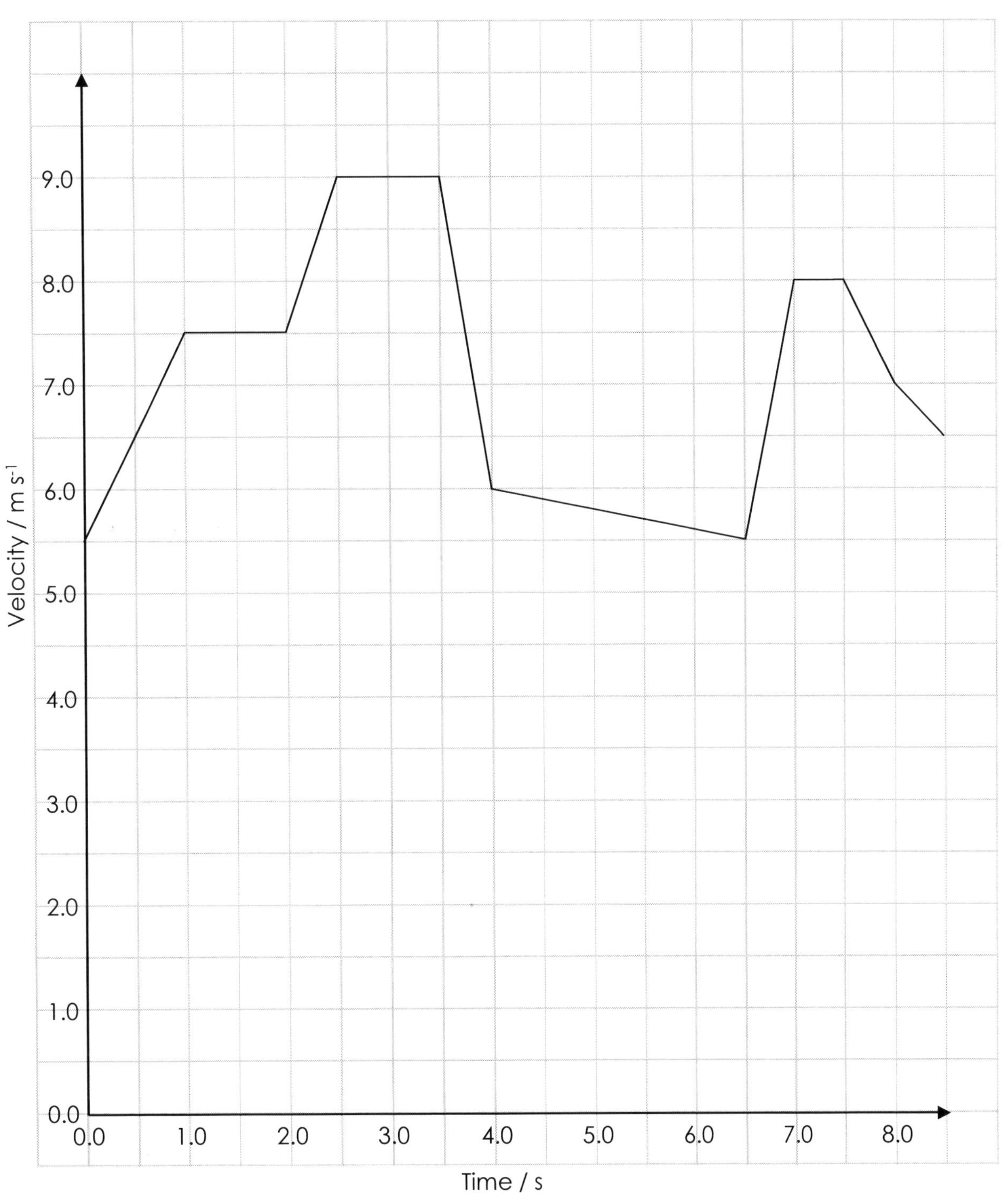

3rd November

1 2

Percentage Uncertainty – Single Measurement

The percentage uncertainty for a single measurement can be calculated from the absolute uncertainty (which is often stated in exam questions) and the measured value.

$$\textit{percentage uncertainty} = \frac{\textit{absolute uncertainty}}{\textit{measured value}} \times 100\%$$

Example: Calculate the percentage uncertainty in the length of a pencil measured with a value of 12.2 ± 0.1 cm.

$$\textit{percentage uncertainty} = \frac{0.1}{12.2} \times 100\% = 0.820 \approx 0.82\ \%\ (2\ \text{s.f.})$$

1. Calculate the **percentage uncertainty** (to 2 s.f.) in the following data:

	Measured Value	Absolute Uncertainty	Percentage Uncertainty / %
a.	15 mm	± 1 mm	
b.	272 mm	± 1 mm	
c.	8.21 s	± 0.01 s	
d.	8.21 s	± 0.2 s	
e.	2.8 kg	± 0.1 kg	
f.	2.802 kg	± 0.001 kg	

2. Determine the **amplitude** and **time period** of the following wave.

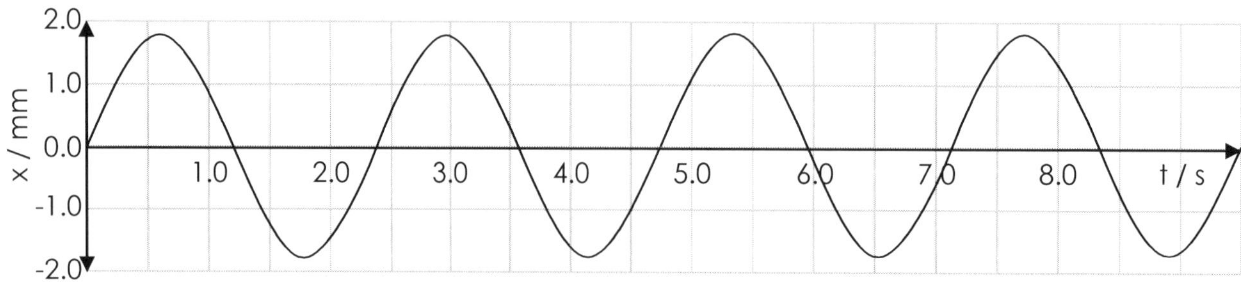

4th November

1 2 3

1. Calculate the **percentage uncertainty** (to 2 s.f.) in the following data:

	Measured Value	Absolute Uncertainty	Percentage Uncertainty / %
a.	10 mm	± 1 mm	
b.	10.14 mm	± 0.01 mm	
c.	8.2 cm	± 1 mm	
d.	0.882 m	± 1 mm	
e.	0.8 s	± 0.1 s	
f.	8.2 s	± 0.1 s	

2. **Define** Ohm's law.

3. Determine the **amplitude**, **time period** and **frequency** of the following wave.

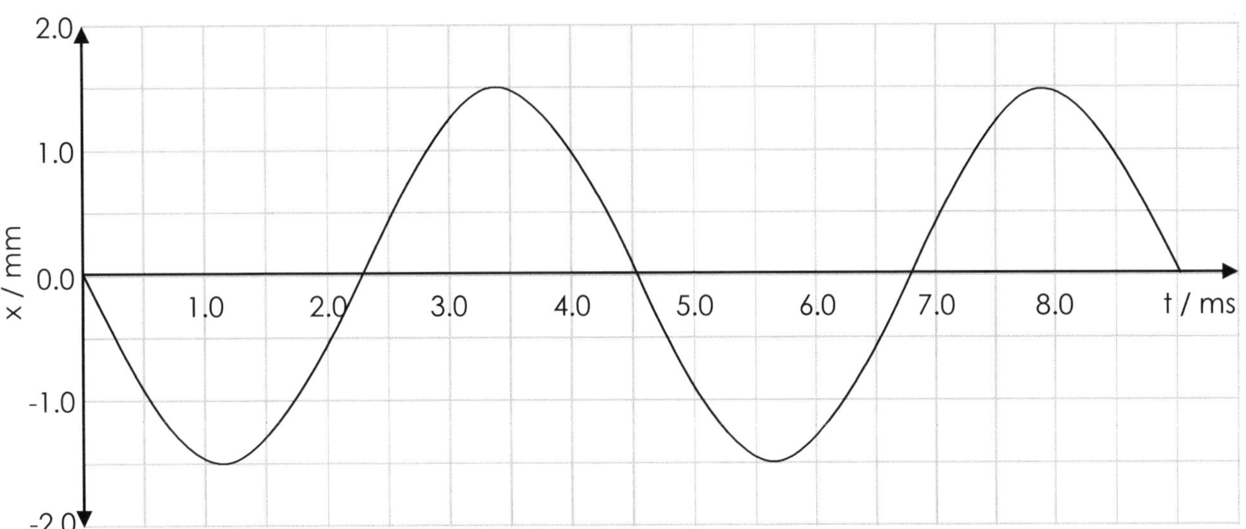

5th November

1 2 3

1. Calculate the **angle**, θ, in a triangle with a hypotenuse of length 6.5 cm and an adjacent side length of 3.1 cm.

2. When investigating resistivity, a wire is used that has its diameter of 0.42 mm measured with a micrometer to ± 0.01 mm, and length of 40.0 cm measured with an uncertainty of ± 1 mm.

   Calculate the **percentage uncertainty** (to 2 s.f.) in:

   a. The **diameter**

   b. The **length**

3. Determine the **amplitude** (in V) and **time period** of the signal on this oscilloscope trace.

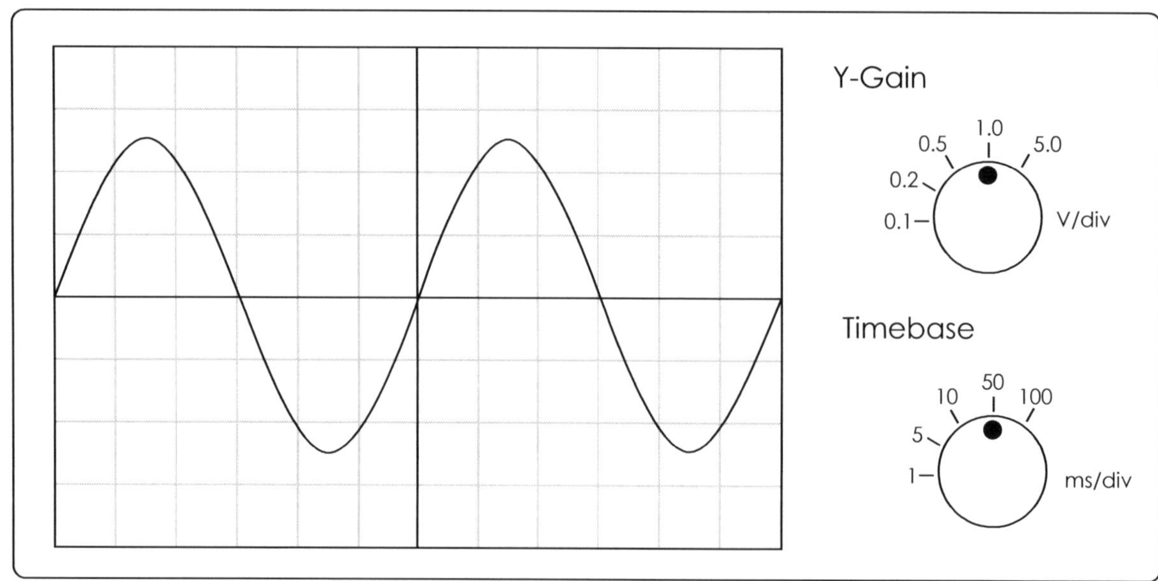

6th November

1 2 3

1. Calculate the **length** of the adjacent side of a right angle triangle with an angle of 10° and an opposite side length of 9.3 cm.

2. Laser light is incident on a double slit and projected onto a screen. The total distance across eleven fringes of light is measured with a ruler as 5.4 cm, with an uncertainty of ± 1 mm.

(not to scale)

   a. Calculate the **percentage uncertainty** (to 2 s.f.) in the distance measured

   b. Calculate the **spacing** between each fringe

   c. State the **percentage uncertainty** in spacing between fringes

3. Define:

   a. **Wavelength**

   b. **Monochromatic light**

   c. **Coherent waves**

7th November

1 2 3

1. Calculate the **mean value**, and **range**, of the following numbers:

	Value 1	Value 2	Value 3	Value 4	Value 5	Mean	Range
a.	82.57	85.48	86.06	85.76	85.29		
b.	17.94	16.82	16.23	16.28	16.57		
c.	9.95	8.04	9.32	8.56	9.00		
d.	3.50	3.57	3.62	3.41	3.43		

2. The wavelength of light is investigated using a double slit. The slit separation is measured using a travelling microscope as 0.60 ± 0.01 mm.

   Calculate the **percentage uncertainty** (to 2 s.f.) in this measurement.

3. Determine the **amplitude** (in V) and **frequency** of the signal on this oscilloscope trace.

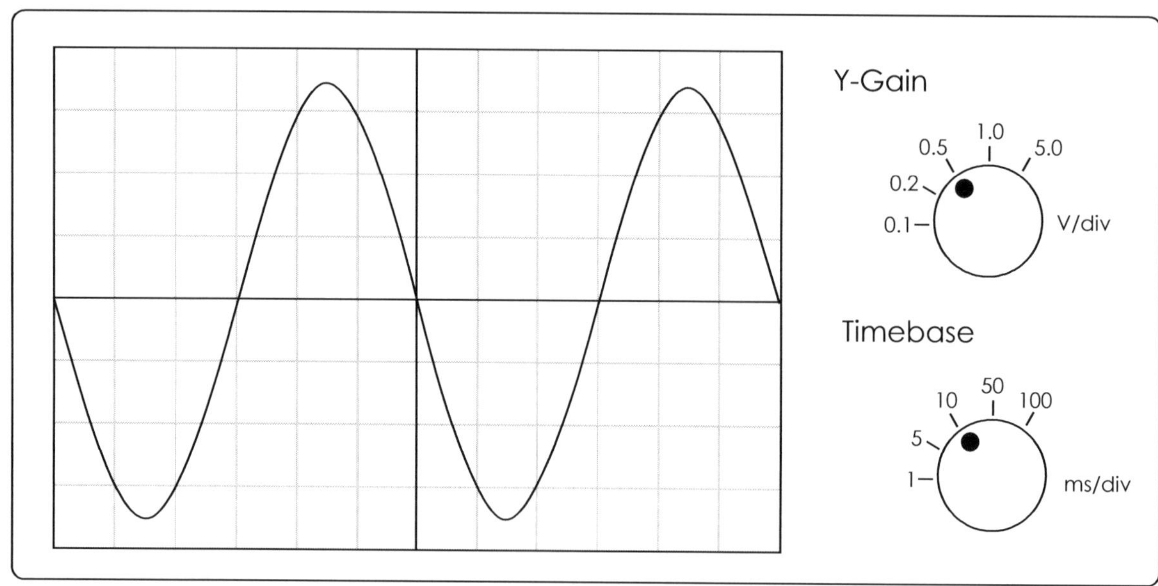

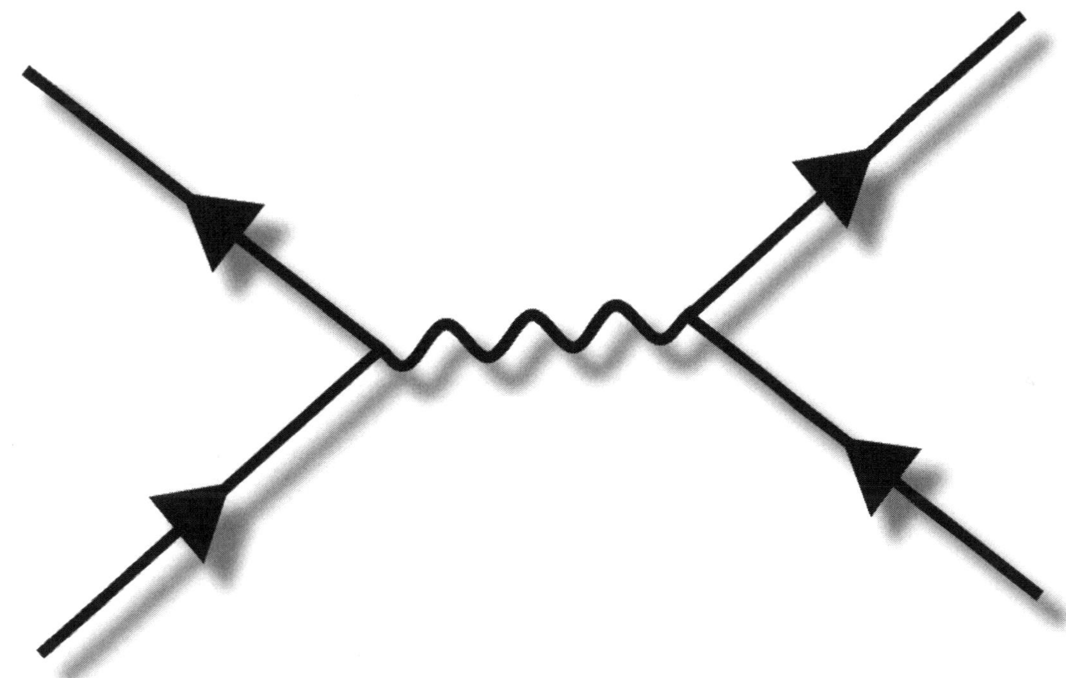

8th November

1 2 3

1. Calculate the **mean value**, and **range**, of the following numbers:

	Value 1	Value 2	Value 3	Value 4	Value 5	Mean	Range
a.	83.53	84.85	86.06	82.66	85.29		
b.	84.35	84.46	84.56	84.47	84.55		
c.	1.85	1.04	1.32	1.56	1.23		
d.	23.53	23.47	23.61	23.14	23.40		

2. To investigate the Young modulus of a material like copper, a thin piece of wire can be loaded so it extends.

   The diameter of wire used in this experiment is measured with a micrometer screw gauge as 0.42 ± 0.01 mm.

   a. Calculate the **percentage uncertainty** (to 2 s.f.) in the diameter

   b. State the **percentage uncertainty** (to 2 s.f.) in the radius

3. A ball is thrown vertically up into the air with an initial velocity of 5.0 m s^{-1}. Calculate how **long** the ball takes to return to the start position.

   State any assumptions made in your answer.

9th November

1 2

Percentage Uncertainty – Repeat Measurements

The percentage uncertainty for repeated measurements can be calculated from the uncertainty, which is equal to half the range, and the mean value.

$$\text{percentage uncertainty} = \frac{\text{half the range}}{\text{mean value}} \times 100\%$$

Example: Calculate the percentage uncertainty in the following set of data:

d / mm	23.4	22.9	23.1	23.3

$\text{half the range} = (23.4 - 22.9) \div 2 = 0.25$

$\text{mean value} = (23.4 + 22.9 + 23.1 + 23.3) \div 4 = 23.175$

$$\text{percentage uncertainty} = \frac{0.25}{23.175} \times 100\% = 1.08 \approx 1.1\% \text{ (2 s.f.)}$$

1. Calculate the **percentage uncertainty** (to 2 s.f.) in the following data:

	Value 1 / mm	Value 2 / mm	Value 3 / mm	Value 4 / mm	Value 5 / mm	Mean / mm	½ Range / mm	Percentage Uncertainty / %
a.	83	84	87	81	86			
b.	83	85	84	84	85			
c.	1.35	1.24	1.32	1.36	1.23			
d.	0.25	0.24	0.26	0.21	0.23			

2. A cheetah accelerates from rest to a velocity of 22 m s^{-1} in a time of 3.5 seconds.

   Calculate how **far** it has travelled in this time.

10th November

1 2 3

1. Calculate the **percentage uncertainty** (to 2 s.f.) of the following data:

	Value 1 / mm	Value 2 / mm	Value 3 / mm	Value 4 / mm	Value 5 / mm	Mean / mm	½ Range / mm	Percentage Uncertainty / %
a.	127	130	132	128	128			
b.	138	135	84	136	132			
c.	2.65	2.68	2.68	2.66	2.64			
d.	0.61	0.61	0.62	0.65	0.63			

2. Define:

   a. **Kirchhoff's first** law

   b. **Kirchhoff's second** law

3. You are given the equation 'energy = momentum x the speed of light'. Work out whether this is **homogeneous** or not.

   Note: An equation is homogenous if the units on both sides of the equals sign are the same.

11th November

1 2 3

1. Define a:

   a. **Progressive** wave

   b. **Transverse** wave

2. While investigating standing waves on a string, the distance between adjacent nodes was measured as 22.0 cm with an uncertainty of ± 0.4 cm owing to the difficulty in identifying exactly where the position of each node was.

   a. Calculate the **percentage uncertainty** (to 2 s.f.) in this measurement.

   b. State the **percentage uncertainty** in the calculated wavelength of the standing wave (the distance from a node to a node is equal to half the wavelength).

3. A van of mass 4500 kg undergoes a collision where it decelerates from an initial velocity of 12.0 m s^{-1} to a final velocity of 4.0 m s^{-1} in a time of 400 ms.

   Calculate the **average force** experienced during the collision.

12th November

1 2 3

1. Determine the **result** that should be recorded for X and calculate the **percentage uncertainty** in the data:

X / mm	0.38	0.42	0.41	0.41	0.42

2. In a further experiment to investigate standing waves on a string, the distance between five nodes was measured as 88.3 cm, again with an absolute uncertainty of ± 0.4 cm owing to the difficulty in identifying exactly where the position of each node was.

   a. Calculate the **percentage uncertainty** (to 2 s.f.) of this measurement

   b. State the **percentage uncertainty** in the calculated wavelength of the standing wave

3. Determine the **amplitude** (in V) and **frequency** of the signal on this oscilloscope trace:

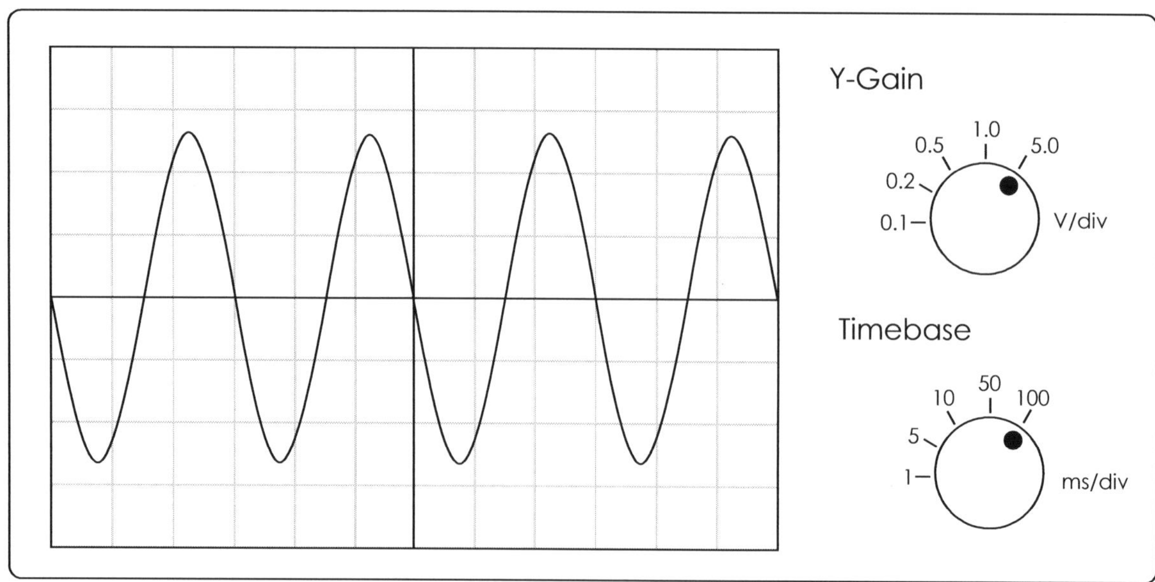

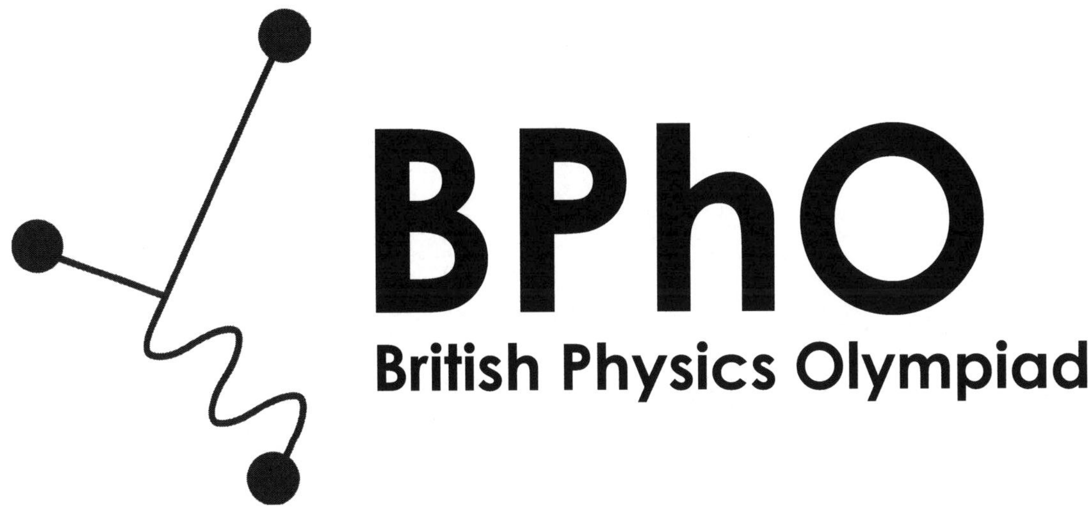

Year 12 - Senior Physics Challenge

This is an opportunity for you to take part in a national physics competition and to develop your confidence in the subject. Ideal for all those who like to engage in problem-solving questions and develop their skills - people like you!

Find out more about the competitions available and how to enter at:

PhysicsOnline.com/**bpho**

13th November

1 2

1. Determine the **result** that should be recorded for the amplitude, A, and calculate the **percentage uncertainty** in the data:

A / cm	9.8	9.4	6.1	9.5	9.4

2. A smooth surface consists of a quarter circle sheet joined onto a smooth horizontal plane. A light, rigid rod with two small, equal masses, m, on each end lies in a vertical plane with the lower mass on the join of the flat and curved surfaces, as shown in the figure below. The separation of the masses is 1/8 of the circumference of the circle.

   When released, the rod and masses will slide along the smooth horizontal plane. Calculate the **maximum speed** if the rod and masses remain in the same vertical plane.

   The radius of the circle is 3.4 m.

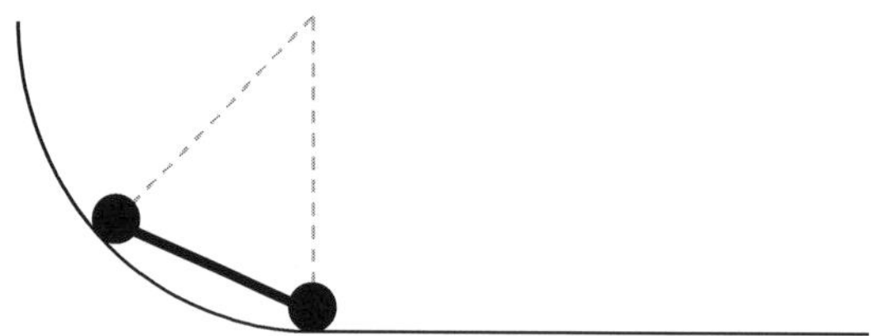

Adapted from a BPhO question from the 2019 Year 12 Challenge

14th November

1 2 3

1. The diameter of a wire, used to measure the Young modulus of copper, was measured in three places with values of 0.42, 0.46 and 0.41 mm.

   Calculate the **mean value** and **percentage uncertainty** (to 2 s.f.) of these measurements.

2. Complete the following **sinusoidal** curve:

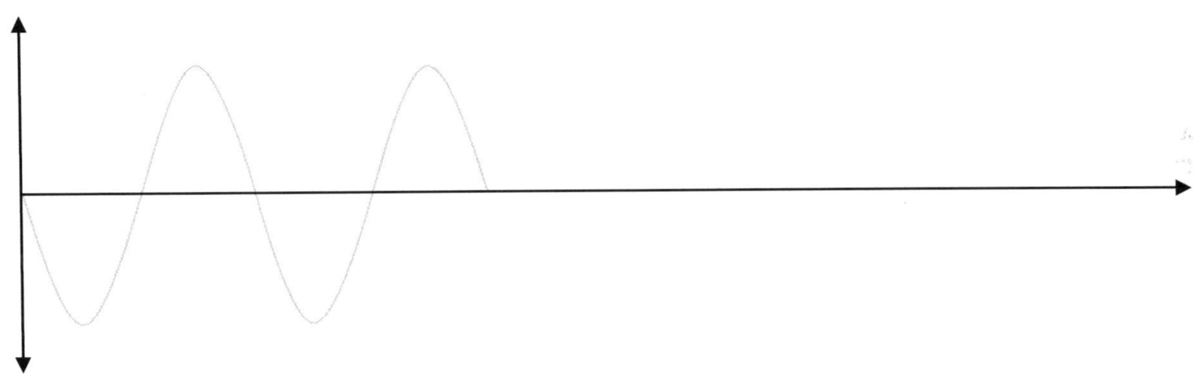

3. Determine the **amplitude** (in V) and **frequency** of the signal on this oscilloscope trace.

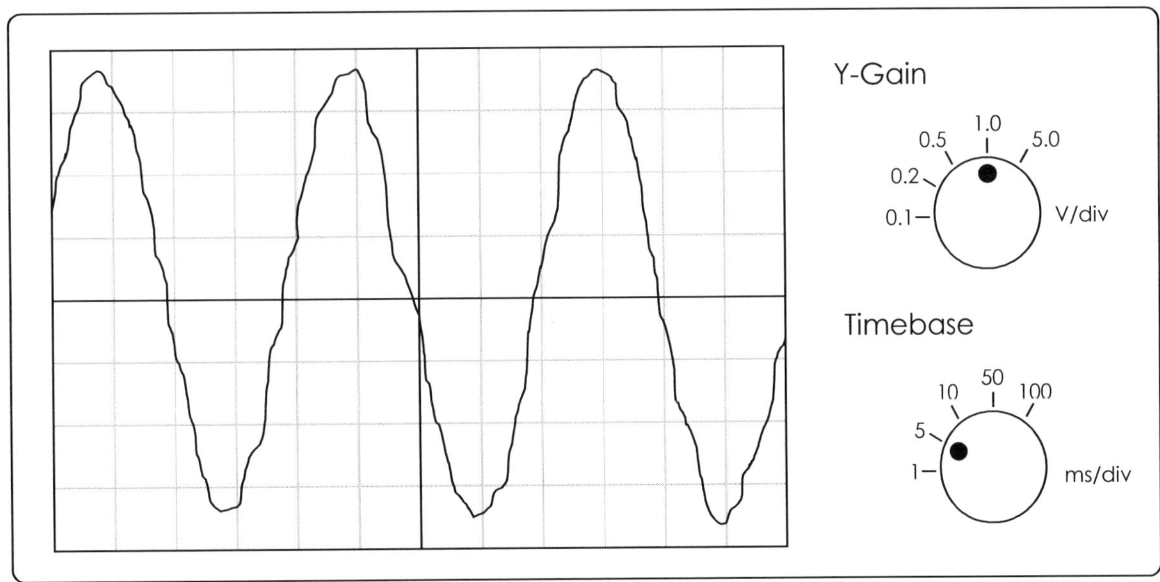

15th November

1 2

Adding Uncertainties

The total uncertainty in a final value can be estimated by adding the absolute uncertainties in the measured values.

$$A = B + C \qquad \Delta A = \Delta B + \Delta C$$

$$A = B - C \qquad \Delta A = \Delta B + \Delta C$$

Note: The uncertainty here has been represented here by 'ΔX'. There is no standard for this at A Level and exam mark schemes give credit for all reasonable methods of working out.

1. The original length of a spring was 5.2 cm. After a tensile load was applied its final length is 8.3 cm. A ruler was used with an uncertainty of ± 1 mm.

   a. State the **absolute uncertainty** in each measurement

   b. Calculate the **extension** of the spring in mm

   c. State the **total uncertainty** in the extension

   d. Calculate the **percentage uncertainty** (to 2 s.f.) in the extension of the spring

2. Write down the definition of **Hooke's law**.

16th November

1 2 3

1. The original length of a wire was 94.2 cm. After a tensile load was applied its final length was 97.1 cm. A ruler was used with an uncertainty of ± 1 mm.
   a. State the **absolute uncertainty** in each measurement
   b. Calculate the **extension** of the wire in mm
   c. State the **total uncertainty** in the extension
   d. Calculate the **percentage uncertainty** (to 2 s.f.) in the extension of the wire

2. Define:
   a. Tensile **stress**
   b. Tensile **strain**
   c. The **Young modulus** of a material

17th November

1 2

1. Convert the following quantities into **SI units**:

   a. 630 nm

   b. 82.3 x 10^{-3} nm

   c. 568 ml

   d. 4.25 ly

   e. 30.0 mph

2. The time taken for a pendulum to make one oscillation was recorded as 0.8 s with an uncertainty estimated to be ± 0.2 s due to human error.

   a. Calculate the **percentage uncertainty** (to 2 s.f.) in this measurement

   To improve the experiment the time taken for ten oscillations was recorded. A value of 8.2 was recorded, with the same uncertainty of ± 0.2 s due to human error.

   b. Calculate the **percentage uncertainty** (to 2 s.f.) in this measurement

   The experiment was carried out by a different group. They recorded the following times from a stopwatch.

t_{10} / s	8.19	8.17	8.07	8.02	8.11

   c. Calculate the **percentage uncertainty** (to 2 s.f.) in this set of data

   d. Comment on your answer

18th November

1. A lever balance, of the same type shown below, can be used to measure the mass of an object.

It consists of two small, unequal pans at the end of a beam balanced on a fulcrum. The arms of the balance are of unequal length, but the beam remains horizontal when the pans are not loaded.

An object of mass M is to be measured. When placed in one pan, the balance is levelled with a mass M_1 in the other pan. When M is placed into other pan, it is balanced by a mass M_2.

a. Find an **expression** that relates M to M_1 and M_2.

M =

b. If M_1 = 1.22 kg and M_2 = 1.90 kg, calculate the **value** of the mass M.

Adapted from a BPhO question from the 2017 Year 12 Challenge

19th November – Part 1

Combining Uncertainties

The total percentage uncertainty in a calculated value can be estimated by combining the percentage uncertainties of the measured values.

$A = BC$	$\%A = \%B + \%C$
$A = BCD$	$\%A = \%B + \%C + \%D$
$A = B/C$	$\%A = \%B + \%C$
$A = B^2$	$\%A = 2 \times \%B$
$A = B^3$	$\%A = 3 \times \%B$
$A = \sqrt{B}$	$\%A = \frac{1}{2} \times \%B$
$A = B^2C/D^3E$	$\%A = (2 \times \%B) + \%C + (3 \times \%D) + \%E$

Note: The percentage uncertainty has been represented here by '%X', this can also be represented by '%U', '%uncertainty' or even 'ε'. There is no standard A Level symbol for this and exam mark schemes give credit for all reasonable methods of working out.

1. Measurements were made to determine the current and potential difference in a circuit component.

Quantity	Percentage Uncertainty
Current	1.8 %
Potential Difference	3.1 %

Calculate the **percentage uncertainty** in the calculated value of:

a. **Resistance**

b. **Power**

19th November – Part 2

2 3

2. Measurements were made to determine the current, potential difference and time in an electrical circuit with a heater.

Quantity	Percentage Uncertainty
Current	4.7 %
Potential Difference	1.7 %
Time	0.2 %

Calculate the **percentage uncertainty** in the calculated value of:

a. **Resistance**

b. **Energy** transferred

3. Measurements were made to determine the diameter, length and resistance of a wire.

Quantity	Percentage Uncertainty
Diameter	2.2 %
Length	0.6 %
Resistance	1.3 %

$$\rho = \frac{RA}{l}$$

Calculate the **percentage uncertainty** in the calculated value of **resistivity**.

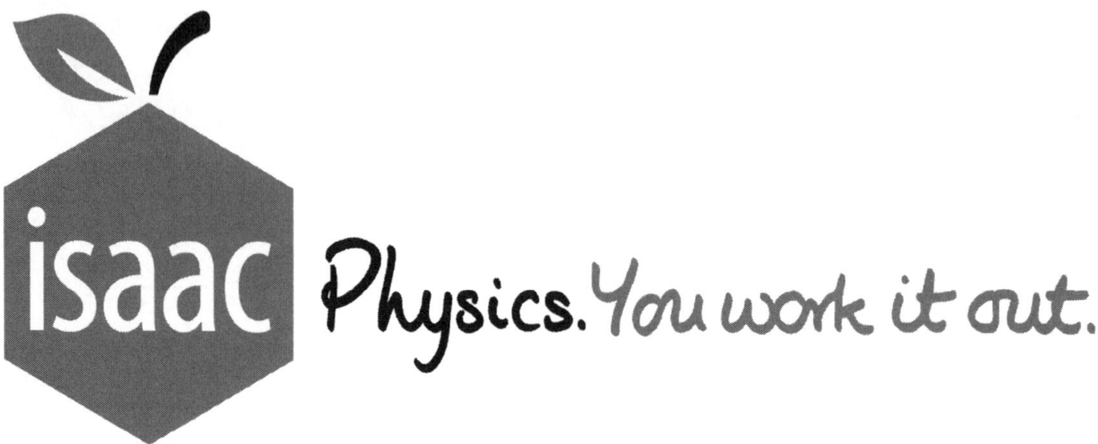

Isaac Physics*

As a teacher I used Isaac Physics all the time with my A Level students and I feel that you should become familiar with it too – it really is an incredible resource.

Thousands of questions to build mastery and develop your problem-solving skills in A Level Physics and beyond. With support on how to solve physics problems and a selection of books with essential skills and linking concepts.

Sign up for an account to track your progress as you enter your answers online.

ALevelPhysicsOnline.com/**isaac-physics**

* This is not a paid advert – this is a recommendation for a free resource I feel you should be aware of.

20th November

1 2 3

1. Determine the **result** that should be recorded for M and calculate the **percentage uncertainty** in the data:

M / kg	0.098	0.101	0.100	0.104	0.098

2. Calculate the **size** and **direction** of the resultant force produced by these two perpendicular forces.

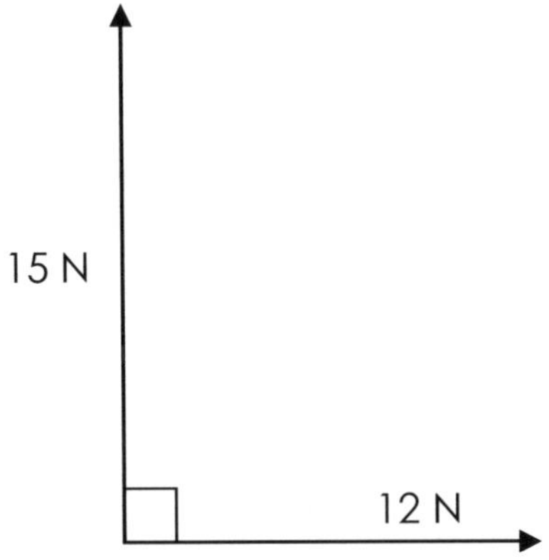

3. Determine the **amplitude** (in V) and **frequency** of the signal on this oscilloscope trace.

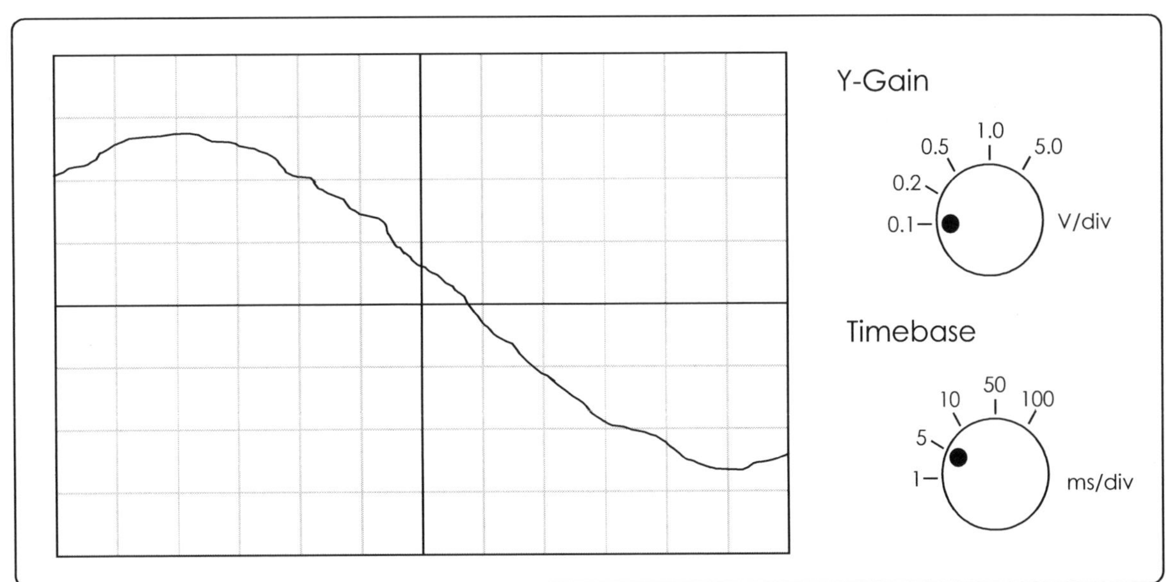

21st November

1 | 2

1. Define:

   a. **Plastic** behaviour

   b. **Elastic** behaviour

2. The resistance of a wire is proportional to its length l, and inversely proportional to its cross-sectional area A. The constant of proportionality, ρ, is known as the resistivity of the material.

$$R = \frac{\rho l}{A}$$

For copper, the resistivity $\rho_{Cu} = 1.68 \times 10^{-8}\ \Omega$ m and for silicon, a semiconductor, with trace amounts of impurities, $\rho_{Si} = 0.53\ \Omega$ m.

The resistance between two opposing faces of a copper cube of length 1.00 m and cross-sectional area 1.00 m^2 is $1.68 \times 10^{-8}\ \Omega$.

Calculate the **length** of the side of a **cube** of silicon with if it had a resistance of $1.68 \times 10^{-8}\ \Omega$ between opposite faces.

Adapted from a BPhO question from the 2016 Year 12 Challenge

22nd November

1 2 3

1. Measurements were made to determine the force on a wire perpendicular to a magnetic field. Calculate the **percentage uncertainty** in the calculated value based on these measurements.

Quantity	Percentage Uncertainty
Magnetic field strength	5.0 %
Current	2.1 %
Length	0.3 %

2. Rearrange the following equation to make '**k**' the subject: $T = 2\pi\sqrt{\frac{m}{k}}$

3. Sketch the **standing/stationary** wave formed on a **string** fixed at both ends:

a. First harmonic

b. Second harmonic

c. Third harmonic

d. Fourth harmonic

23rd November

1 2 3

1. Measurements were made to determine the spring constant on an oscillating mass-spring system. Calculate the **percentage uncertainty** in the calculated value of '**k**' based on these measurements.

Quantity	Percentage Uncertainty
Mass	0.2 %
Time period	1.3 %

$$T = 2\pi\sqrt{\frac{m}{k}}$$

2. Rearrange the following equation to make '**g**' the subject: $T = 2\pi\sqrt{\frac{l}{g}}$

3. Sketch the **standing/stationary** wave formed in the tube open at one end:

   a. First harmonic

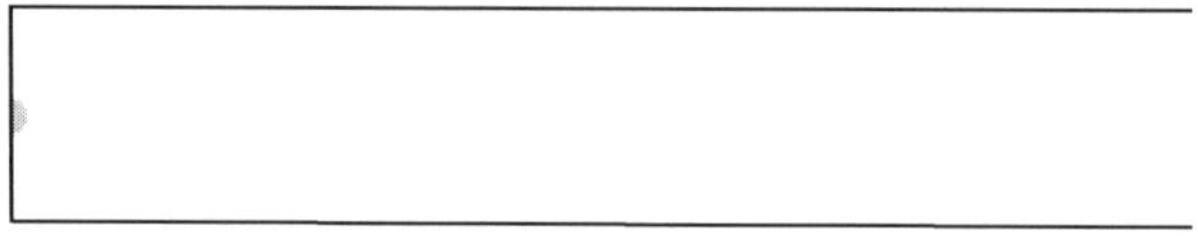

   b. Second harmonic

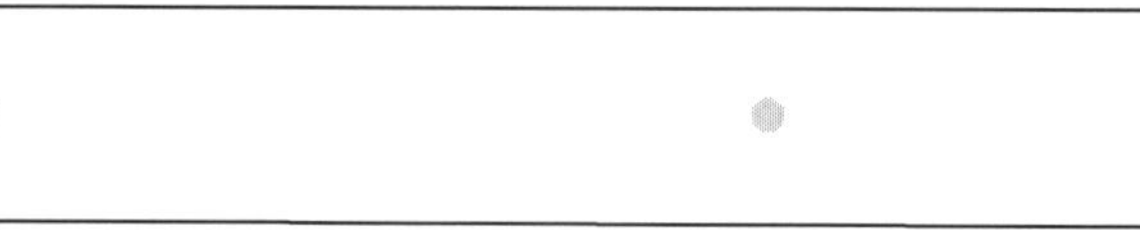

   c. Third harmonic

   d. Fourth harmonic

24th November

1 2 3

1. Measurements were made to determine the gravitational field strength using an oscillating pendulum. Calculate the **percentage uncertainty** in the calculated value of '**g**' based on these measurements.

Quantity	Percentage Uncertainty
Length	1.0 %
Time period	2.3 %

$$T = 2\pi\sqrt{\frac{l}{g}}$$

2. Rearrange $F = 6\pi\eta rv$ to make:

   a. **r** the subject

   b. **v** the subject

   c. **η** the subject

3. Sketch the **standing/stationary** wave formed in a tube open at both ends:

   a. First harmonic

   b. Second harmonic

   c. Third harmonic

   d. Fourth harmonic

25th November – Part 1

1. Draw in a straight **line of best fit** for the following data:

a.

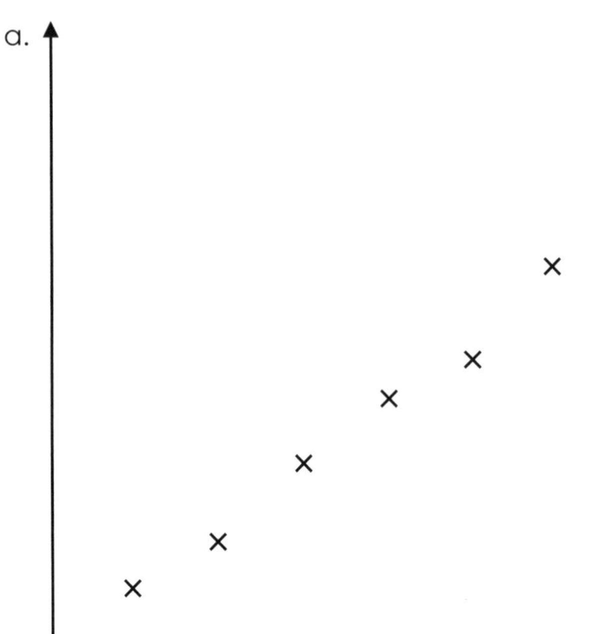

b.

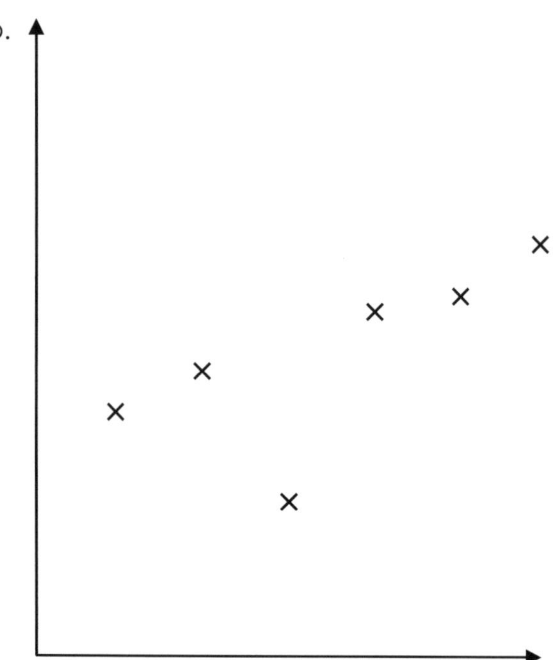

c.

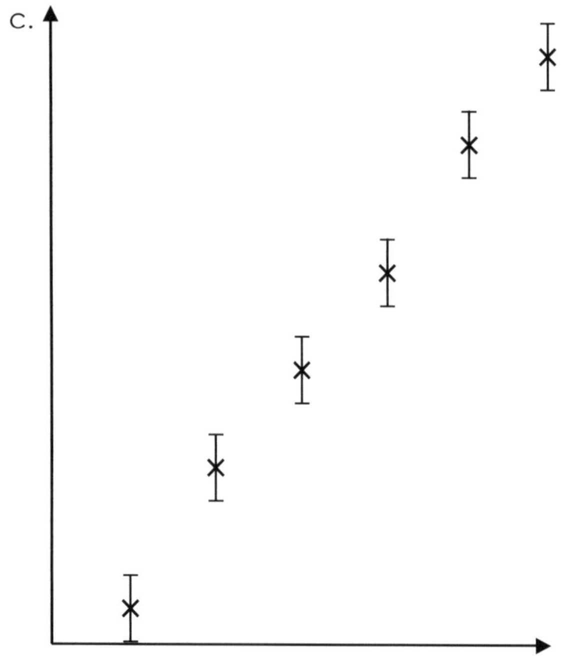

d.

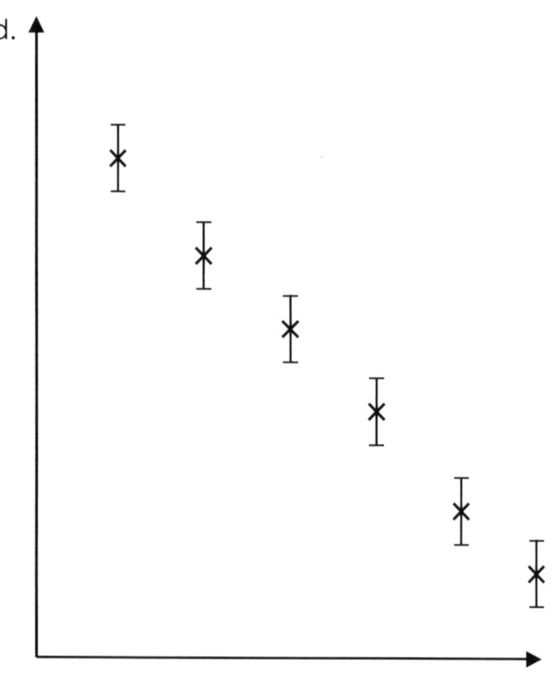

25th November – Part 2

2. The 'line of best fit' has been added to these graphs. Draw in a '**worst acceptable**' line. This must pass through all the error bars for the following data.

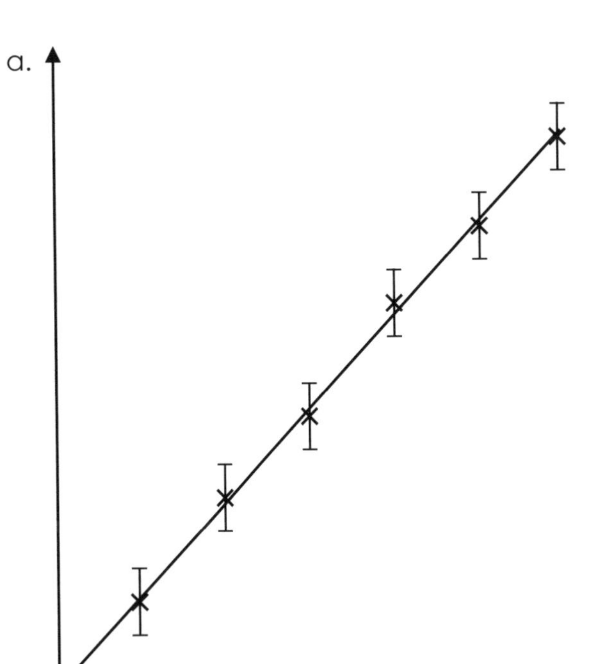

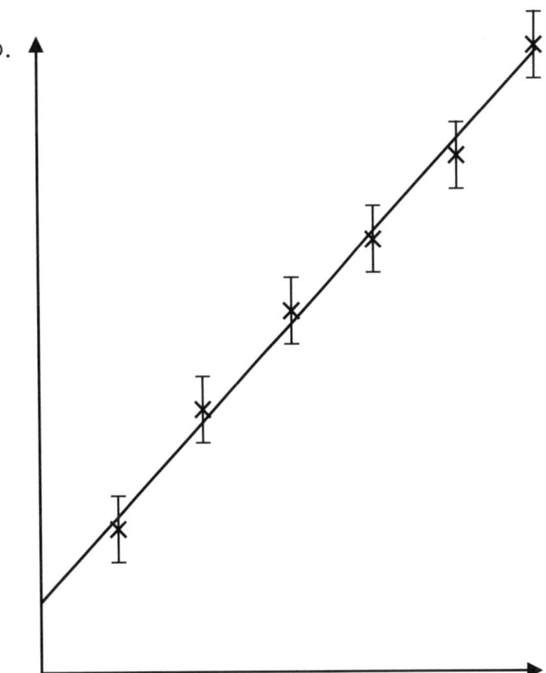

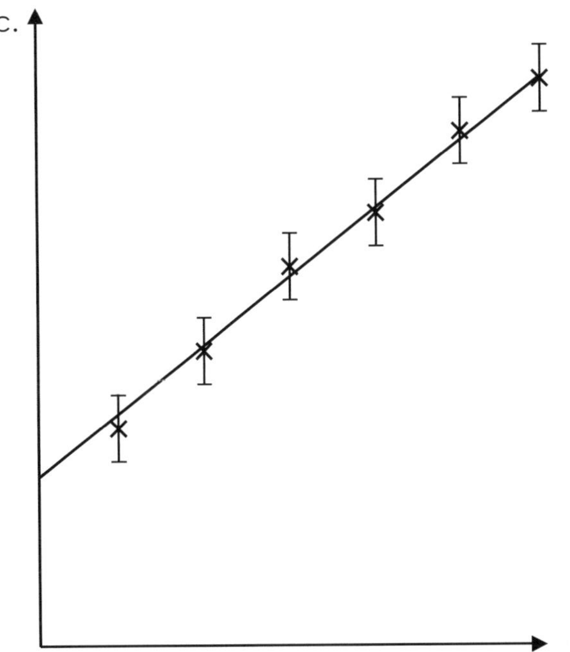

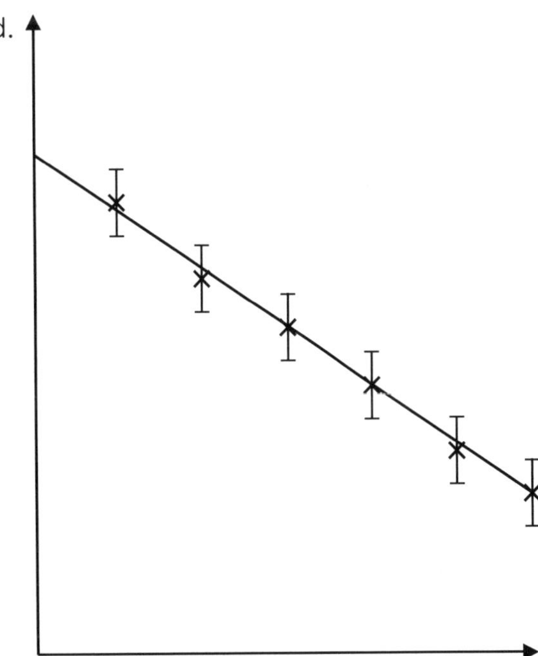

26th November

1 2

1. A solid rectangular block of height 'h' and width 'w' is placed on a plane inclined at an angle θ. Friction prevents the block from sliding down the slope.

   Write down an expression for the **maximum angle** of the slope 'θ_{max}' such that the block will remain upright.

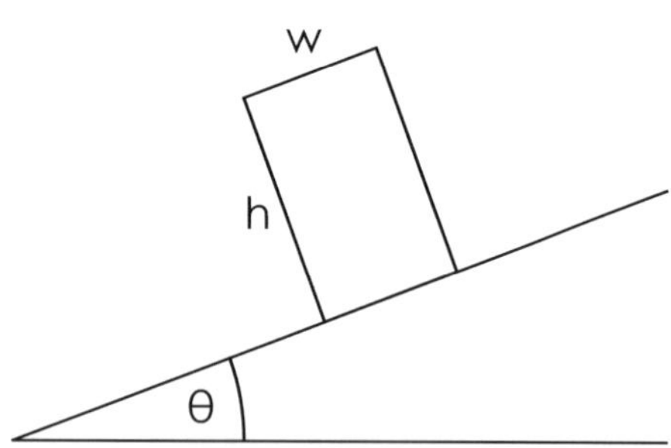

From a BPhO question from the 2015 Year 12 Challenge

2. A massive solid cube of side $l = r\pi/2$, and of uniform density, is placed on the highest point of a cylinder of radius r, as shown below. If the cylinder is rough so that no sliding occurs, calculate the full **range** of the **angle** through which the block can swing (or wobble) without tipping off (you can assume that this range of equilibrium positions is stable).

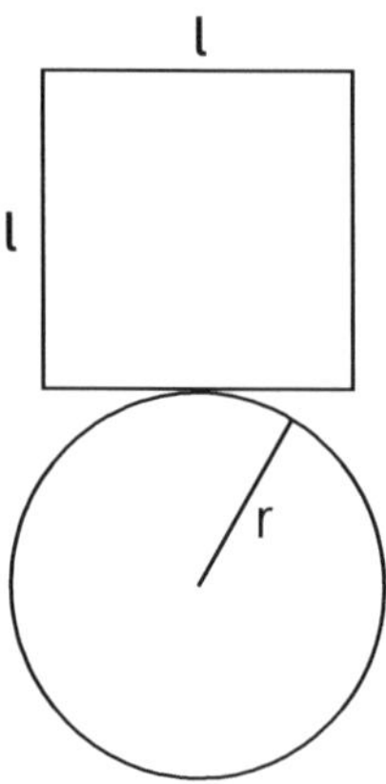

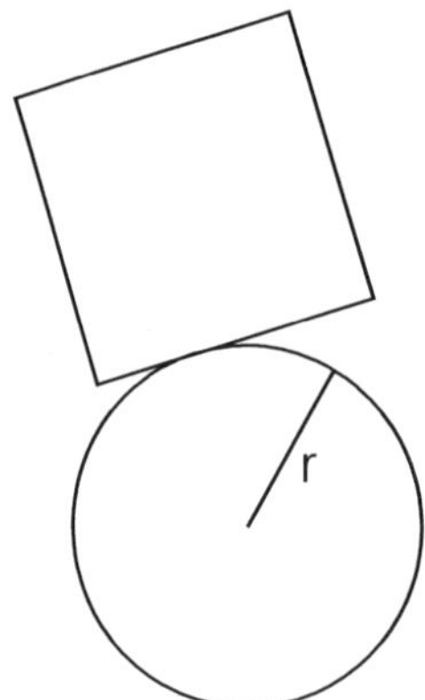

From a BPhO question from the 2015 Year 12 Challenge

27th November

1 2

1. Write the following derived units in terms of their SI Base Units:

   a. **Coulomb**

   b. **Newton**

   c. **Joule**

   d. **Volt**

2. Determine the **amplitude** (in V) and **frequency** of the signal on this oscilloscope trace.

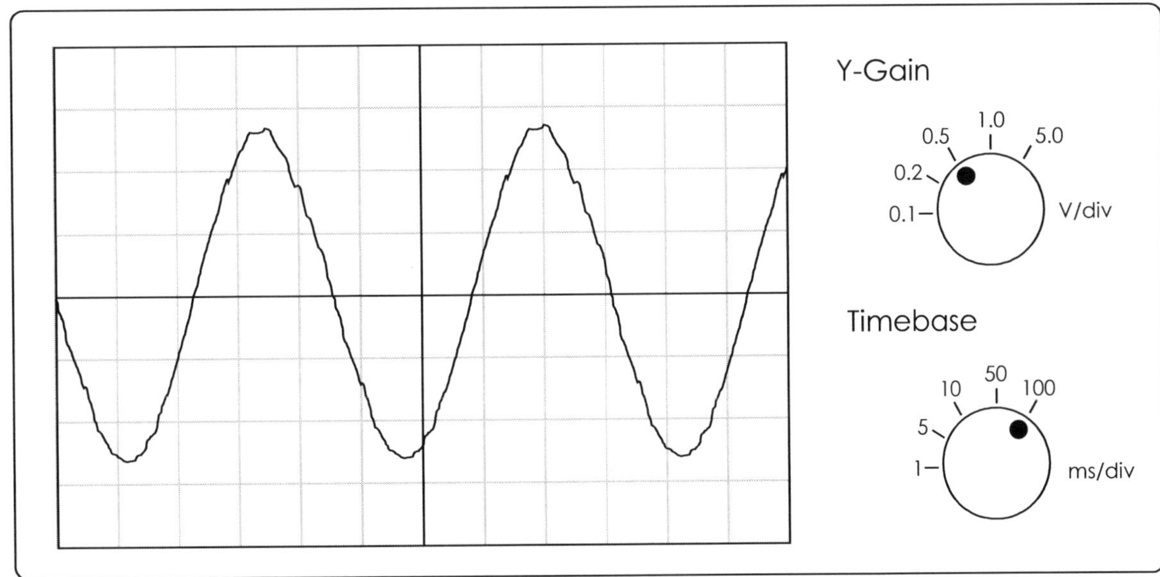

28th November – Part 1

1

1. Draw in a '**worst acceptable**' line. This must pass through the error bars for the following data:

a.

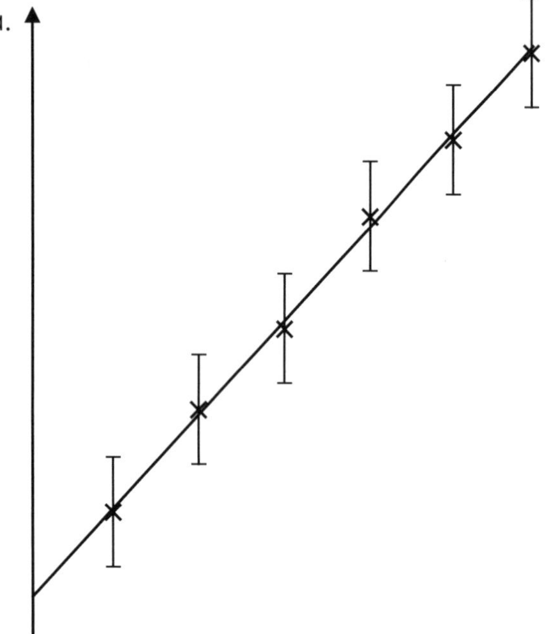

b.

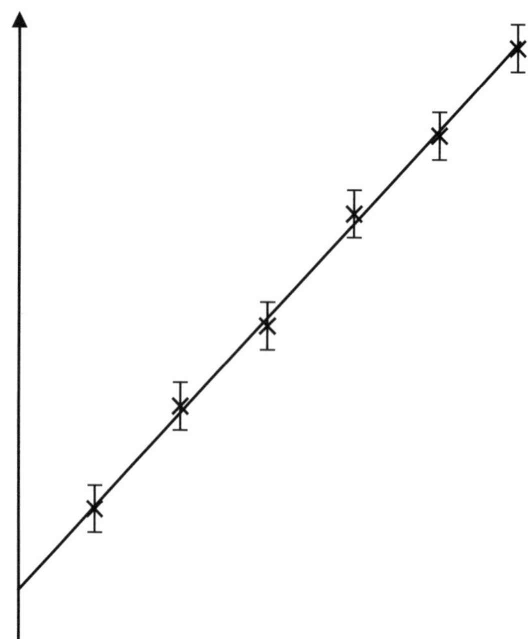

c.

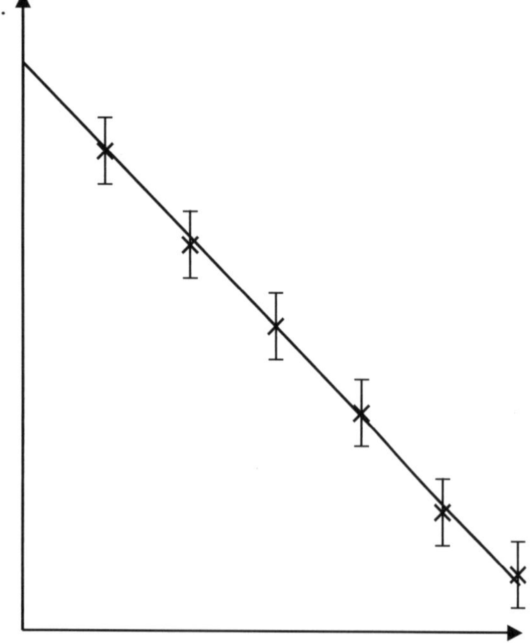

d.

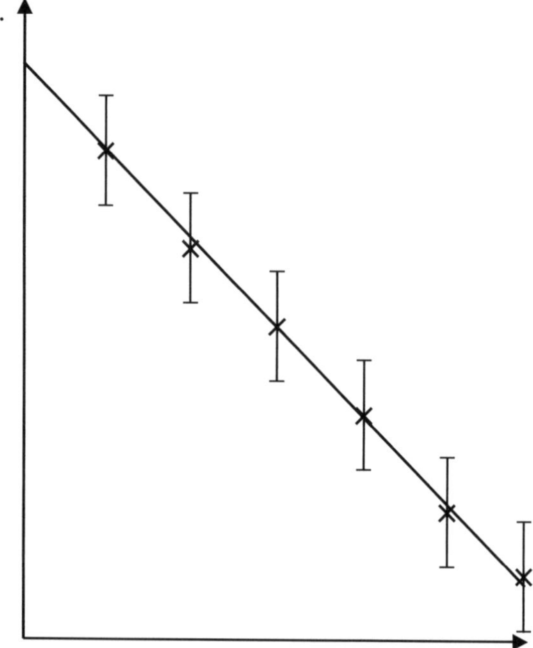

28th November – Part 2

2. Draw in a '**line of best fit**' and a '**worst acceptable**' line that passes through the error bars for the following data:

a.

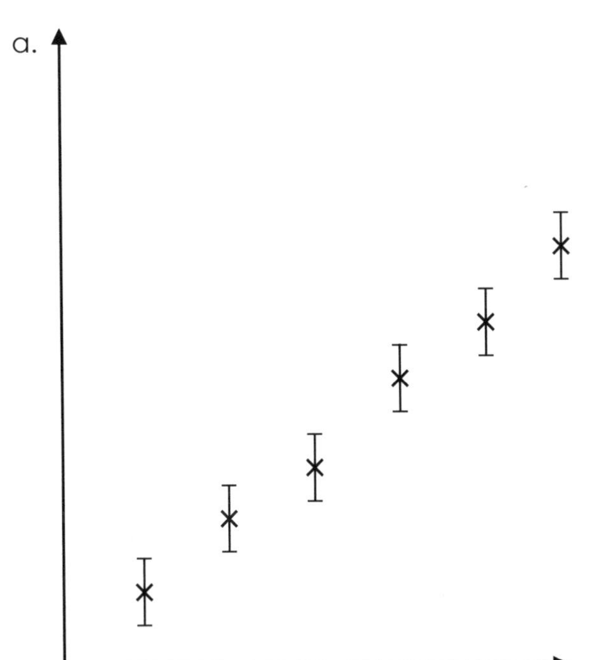

b.

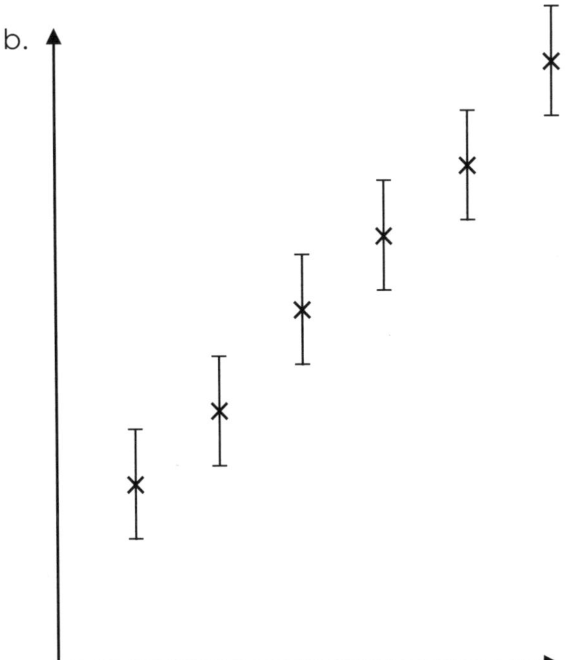

c.

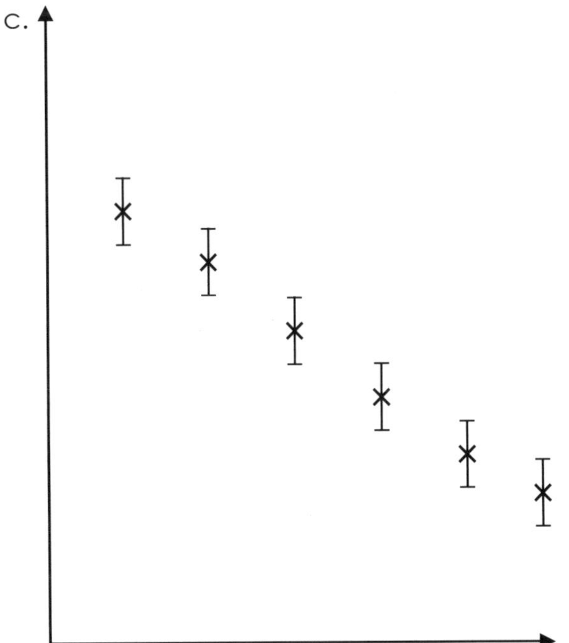

d.

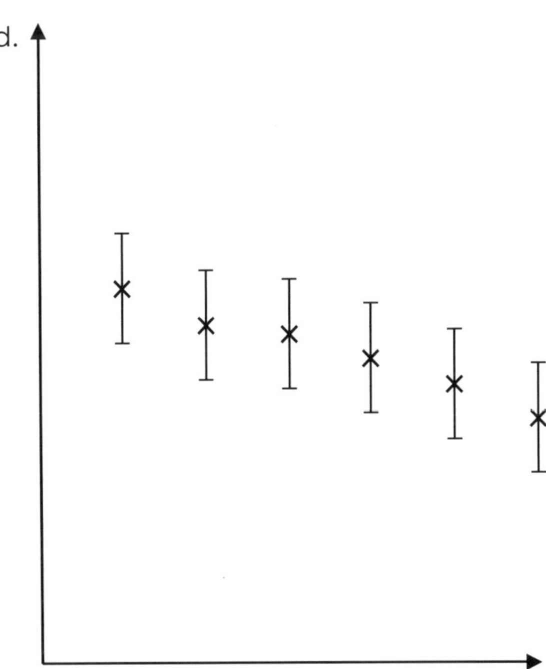

29th November

1. A simple experiment is carried out to find the acceleration due to gravity 'g' by a freefall method. A ball is released from rest through a height measured as 80.0 cm with an uncertainty of ± 1 mm.

   The following times are recorded with a digital stopwatch.

t / s	0.41	0.44	0.40	0.47	0.43

   a. Calculate the **mean value** of 't'

   b. If air resistance is assumed to be negligible, calculate the **value** of 'g' that this data suggests

   c. Calculate the **percentage uncertainty** in the recorded data for height and time

   d. Calculate the **percentage uncertainty** in your final calculated value of 'g'

   e. Calculate the **uncertainty** (in m s^{-2}) in your value for 'g'

30th November

1 2 3

1. Define **equilibrium**.

2. Complete the following **sinusoidal** curve:

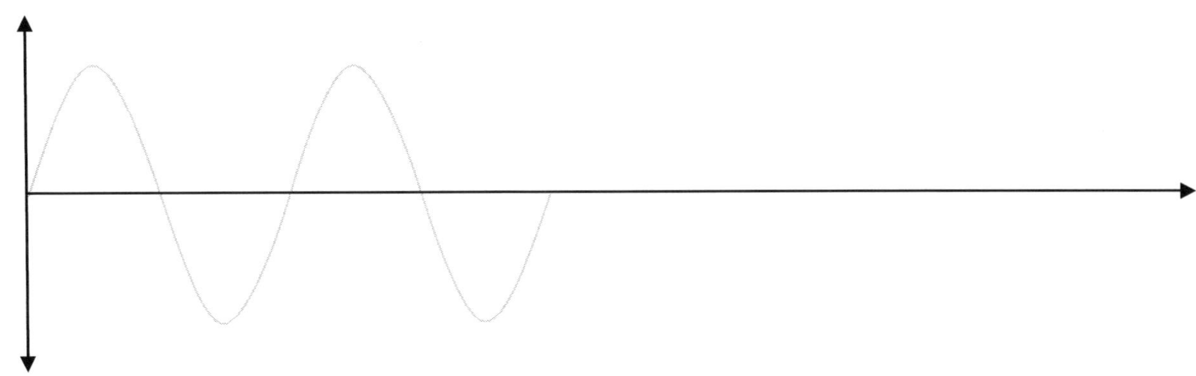

3. Sketch the fundamental frequency of **standing** wave formed below:

   a. **String** fixed at both ends

   b. Tube open at **one** end

   c. Tube open at **both** ends

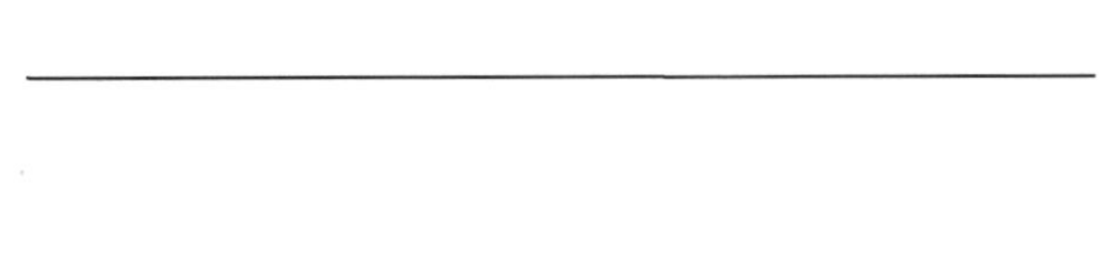

NOVEMBER REVIEW

Record your progress at the end of the month and have another go at any questions you may have missed.

A Level Physics Content	Red	Amber	Green
I can calculate **percentage uncertainty** for a **single measurement**.			
I can calculate **percentage uncertainty** for **repeat measurements**.			
I can spot **anomalous** data in tabulated results.			
I can **add uncertainties** to work out the total absolute uncertainty in a measured value.			
I can **combine uncertainties** to work out the total uncertainty in a calculated value.			
I can read an **oscilloscope**.			

Any other comments:

DECEMBER

DECEMBER

The autumn term is usually the longest term of the academic year. With increased workload and demands on your time this is one of the toughest periods of your A Levels.

In a few weeks you will be on a school holiday with time to unwind and catch up on your rest. Keep this in mind as you continue putting in the work. All that effort will pay off!

1st December

1 2 3

1. State the **principle of moments**.

2. Form **expressions** for p and q in terms of θ and W.

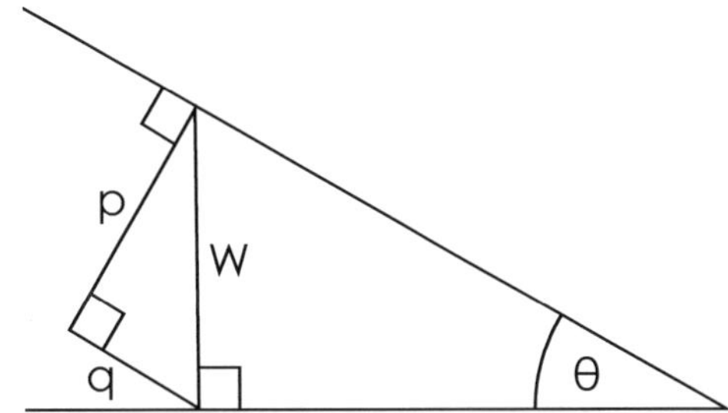

3. A 10 Ω resistor is connected to a 6.0 V battery.

   Calculate the **change in current** drawn from the battery when a 10 Ω resistor is added:

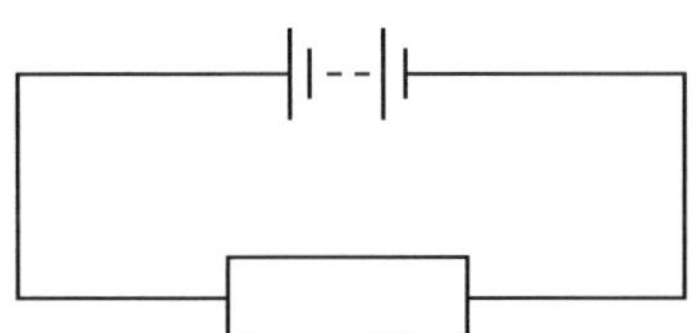

   a. In **series**

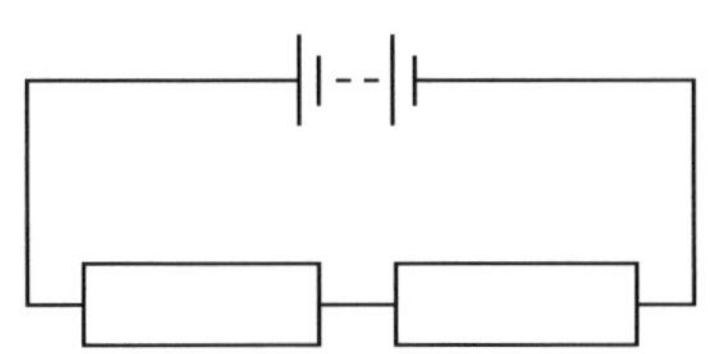

   b. In **parallel**

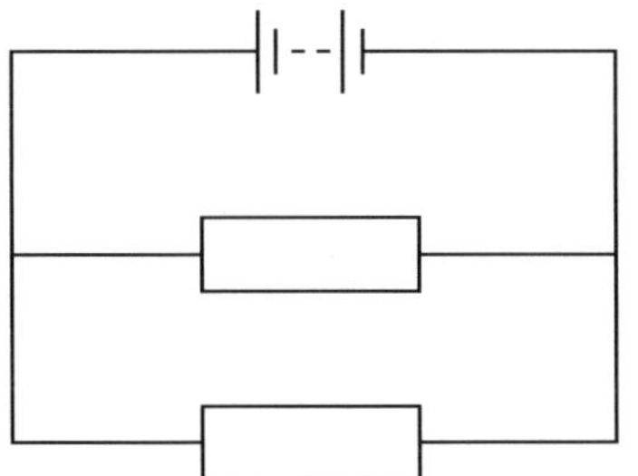

2nd December

1 2 3

1. Define **resistance**.

2. Calculate the **lengths** of p and q when θ = 24° and W = 30.

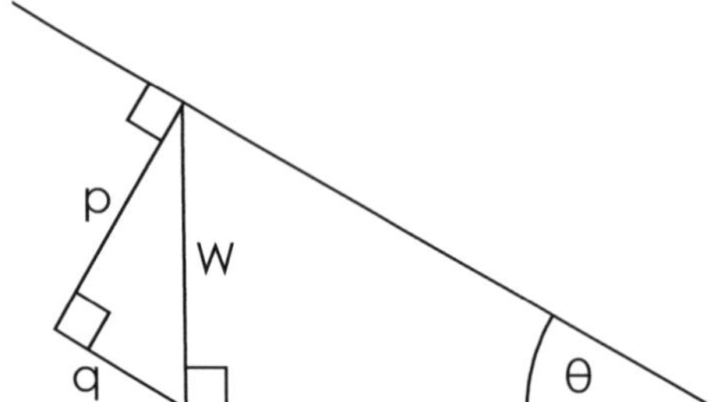

3. The following data was recorded:

Quantity	Value	Uncertainty
Mass	0.250 kg	± 0.001 kg
Velocity	0.337 m s^{-1}	± 0.010 m s^{-1}

Calculate the **percentage uncertainty** in the calculated value of:

a. Momentum

b. Kinetic energy

3rd December

1 2 3

1. Three measurements of the gravitational field strength are made: 9.58 N kg^{-1}, 9.92 N kg^{-1} and 10.14 N kg^{-1}.

   Calculate the **mean** gravitational field strength and its **absolute uncertainty**.

2. A wooden block of weight 5.0 N is at rest on a slope in a Physics classroom at an angle of 17° from the desk.

   Calculate the components of its weight **parallel** and **perpendicular** to the surface.

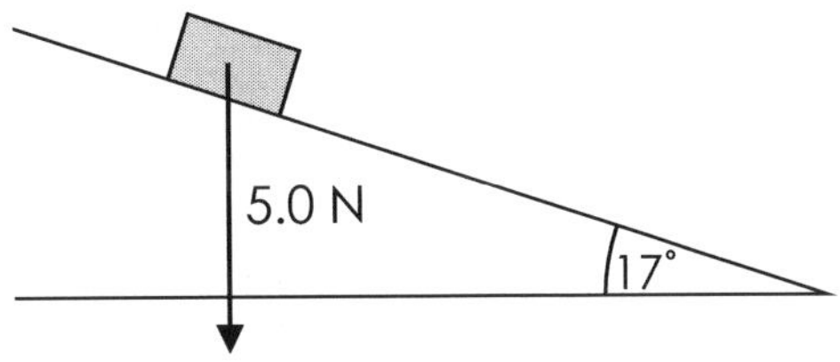

3. Calculate the **gradient** of the line.

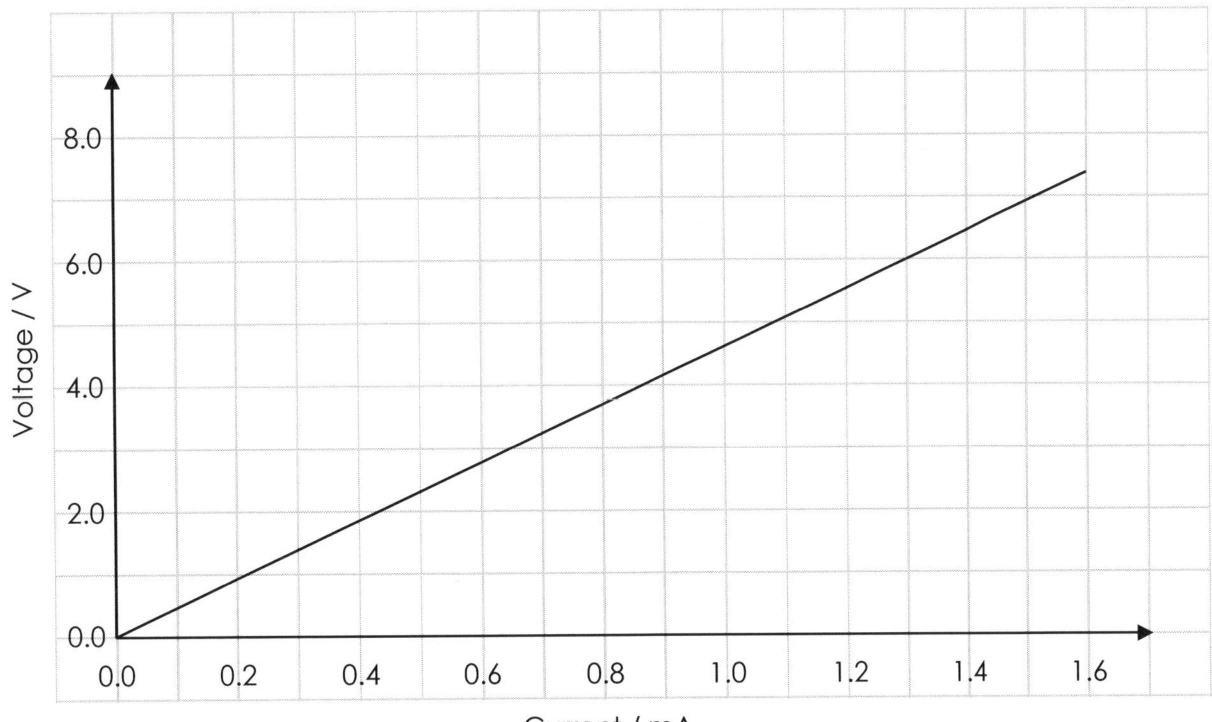

4th December – Part 1

Percentage Uncertainty – Gradient

The percentage uncertainty in the gradient of a straight line graph can be calculated from the line of best fit and the gradient of the worst acceptable line.

$$percentage\ uncertainty = \frac{|gradient_{best} - gradient_{worst}|}{gradient_{best}} \times 100\%$$

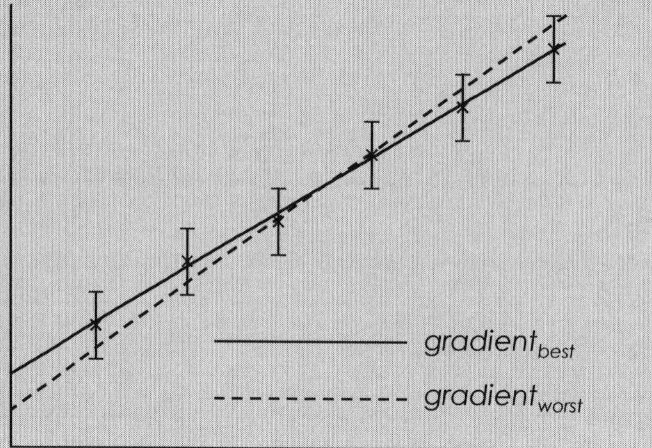

Note: The steepest or shallowest worst acceptable line can be drawn, as the modulus (positive value) is used. If there are error bars on the plotted data then the worst acceptable line should pass through all of these.

1. Complete the following table:

	$Gradient_{best}$	$Gradient_{worst}$	Percentage Uncertainty / %
a.	1.00	1.10	
b.	9.62	9.84	
c.	9.62	9.40	
d.	9.62	8.87	

4th December – Part 2

2. The following data was collected in an A Level practical investigation.

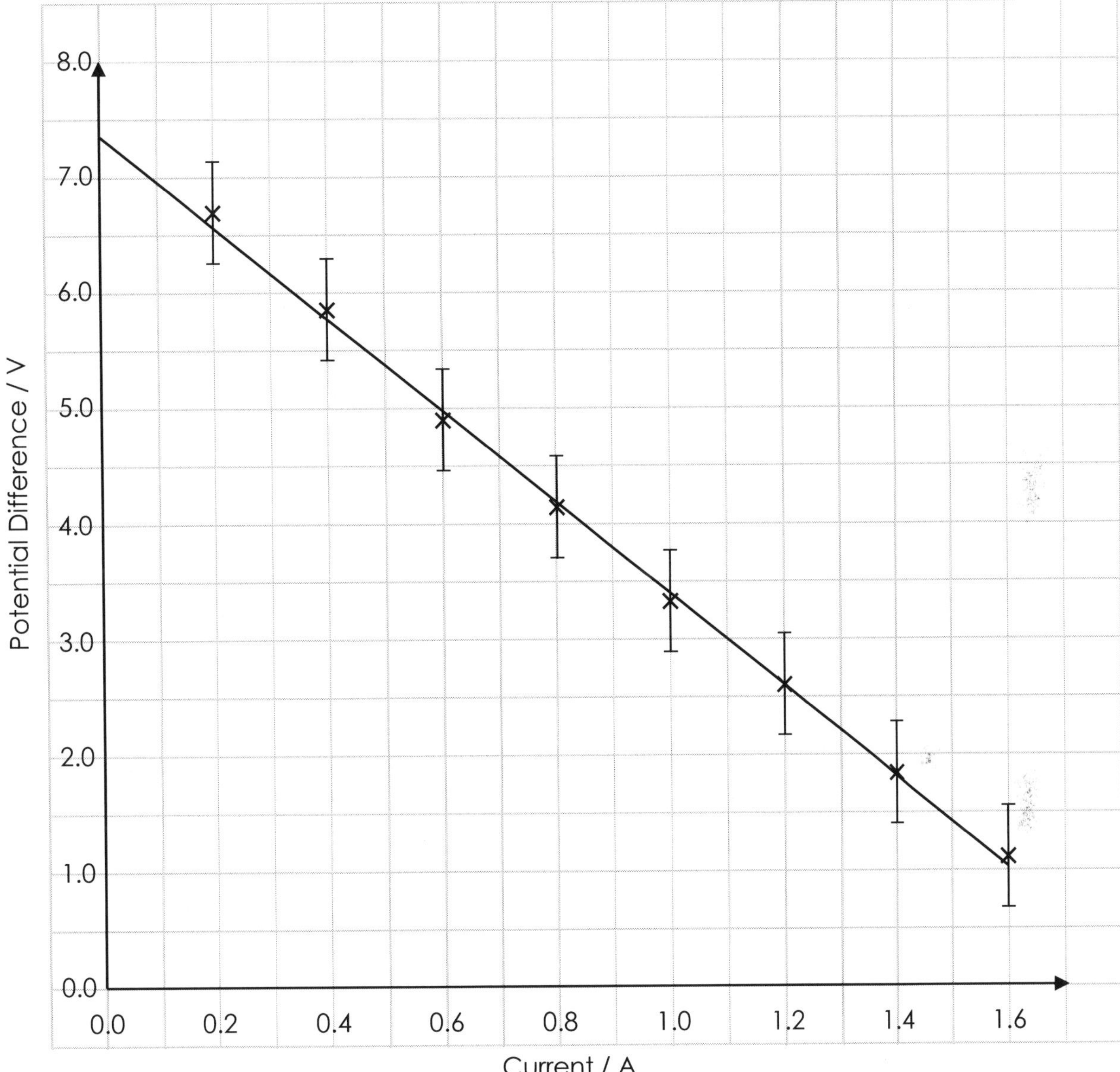

a. Calculate the gradient of the **line of best fit**

b. Draw in a **worst acceptable** line and calculate the **gradient** of this

c. Calculate the **percentage uncertainty** in the gradient

5th December

1 2 3

1. **Convert**:

   a. 1.00 eV to J

   b. 1.00 kWh to J

2. A 2.1 g raindrop runs down an angled window in a roof at a constant velocity of 11 cm s^{-1}.

   Calculate the **normal contact force** and the **drag**.

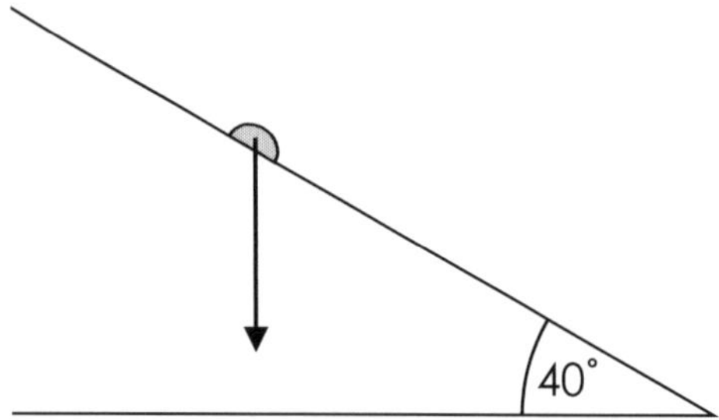

3. A mountain bike, with tyres of outside diameter 29 inches, is travelling at 24 mph.

   1 mile = 1609 m   1 inch = 2.54 cm

   a. Calculate the **speed** of the bike in m s^{-1}

   b. Calculate how many **revolutions** each wheel makes per second

   c. Determine the **speed** of the tyre at the point where it meets the ground

   d. State where the tyre is travelling **fastest**

6th December – Part 1

1. The following data was collected in an A Level practical investigation.

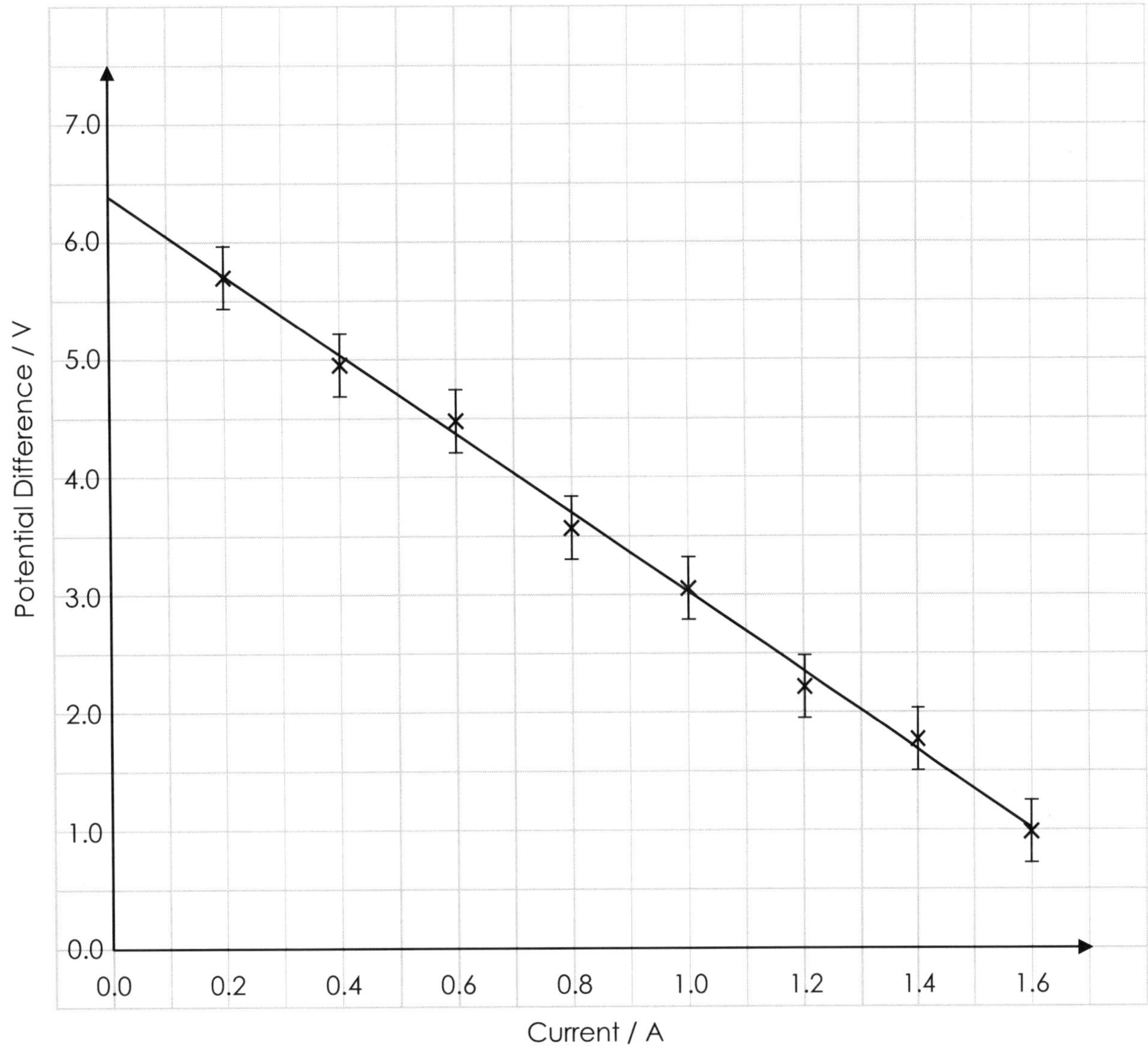

a. Calculate the gradient of the **line of best fit**

b. Draw in a **worst acceptable** line and calculate the **gradient** of this

c. Calculate the **percentage uncertainty** in the gradient

6th December – Part 2

2. The following data was collected in an A Level practical investigation.

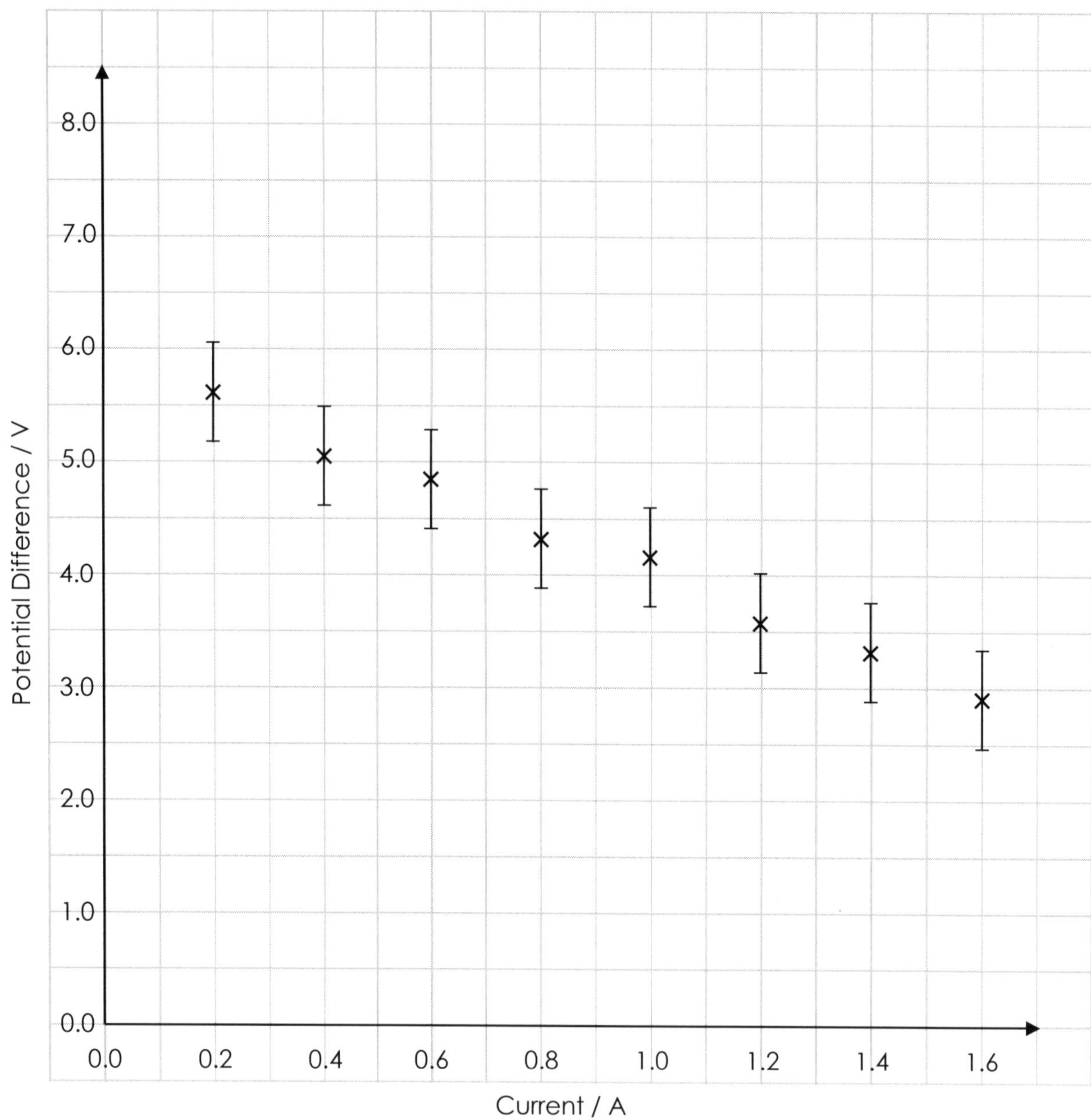

By drawing your own line of best fit and worst acceptable line, calculate the **percentage uncertainty** in the **gradient.**

7th December – Part 1

Percentage Uncertainty – y-intercept

The percentage uncertainty in the y-intercept of a straight line graph can be calculated from the line of best fit and the intercept of the worst acceptable line.

$$\text{percentage uncertainty} = \frac{|\text{y-intercept}_{best} - \text{y-intercept}_{worst}|}{\text{y-intercept}_{best}} \times 100\%$$

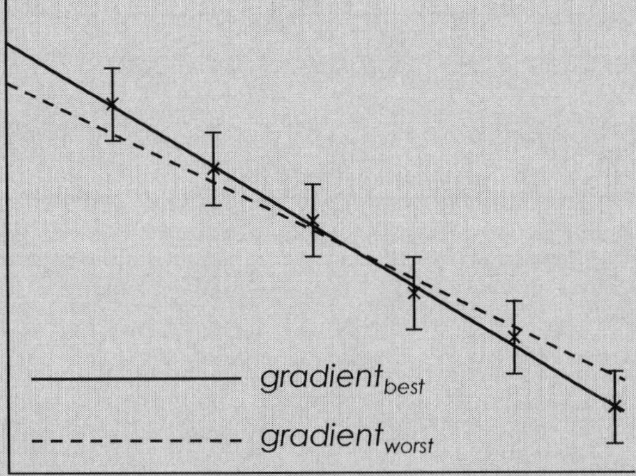

Note: The steepest or shallowest worst acceptable line can be used. If there are error bars on the plotted data then the worst acceptable line should pass through all of these.

1. Complete the following table:

	Y-intercept$_{best}$	Y-intercept$_{worst}$	Percentage Uncertainty / %
a.	1.00	1.10	
b.	6.0	6.2	
c.	6.0	5.6	
d.	42.0	38.5	

7th December – Part 2

2. The following data was collected in an A Level practical investigation.

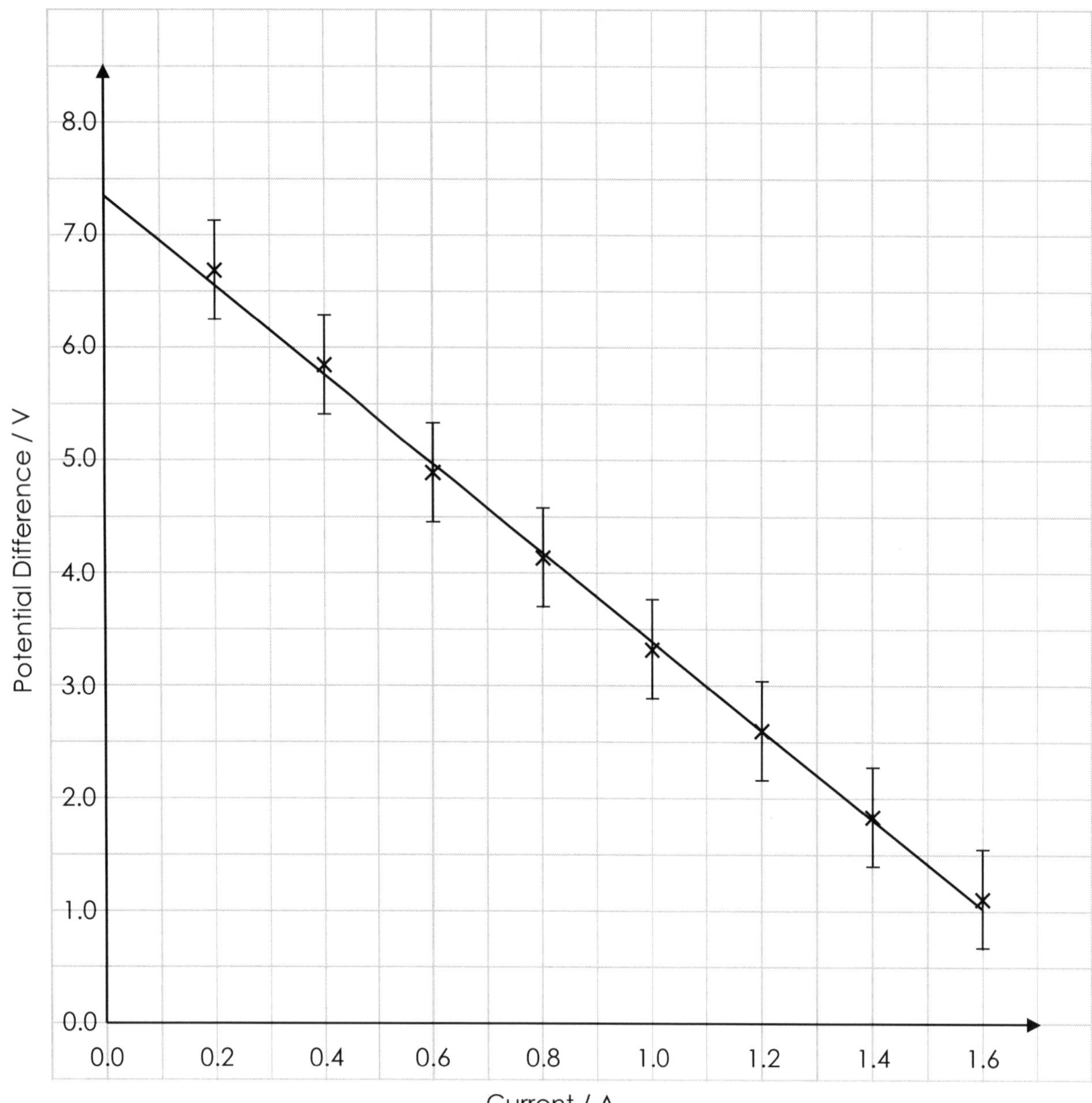

The y-intercept of the line of best fit is equal to 7.3 V.

a. Draw in a **worst acceptable** line and determine the **y-intercept** of this line

b. Calculate the **percentage uncertainty** in the y-intercept

8th December

1 2 3

1. **Convert**:
   a. 1.00 J to eV

   b. 1.00 J to kWh

2. **Estimate** the:
   a. Mass of an adult male human

   b. The speed of a runner

   c. The mass of a family car

   d. The kinetic energy of a running cat

3. An L16 81 mm mortar is fired at 225 m s^{-1} at an angle of 70 degrees to the horizontal.

   Calculate how **far** the mortar bomb will travel horizontally before it hits the ground, listing any assumptions made.

9th December – Part 1

1

1. The following data was collected in an A Level practical investigation.

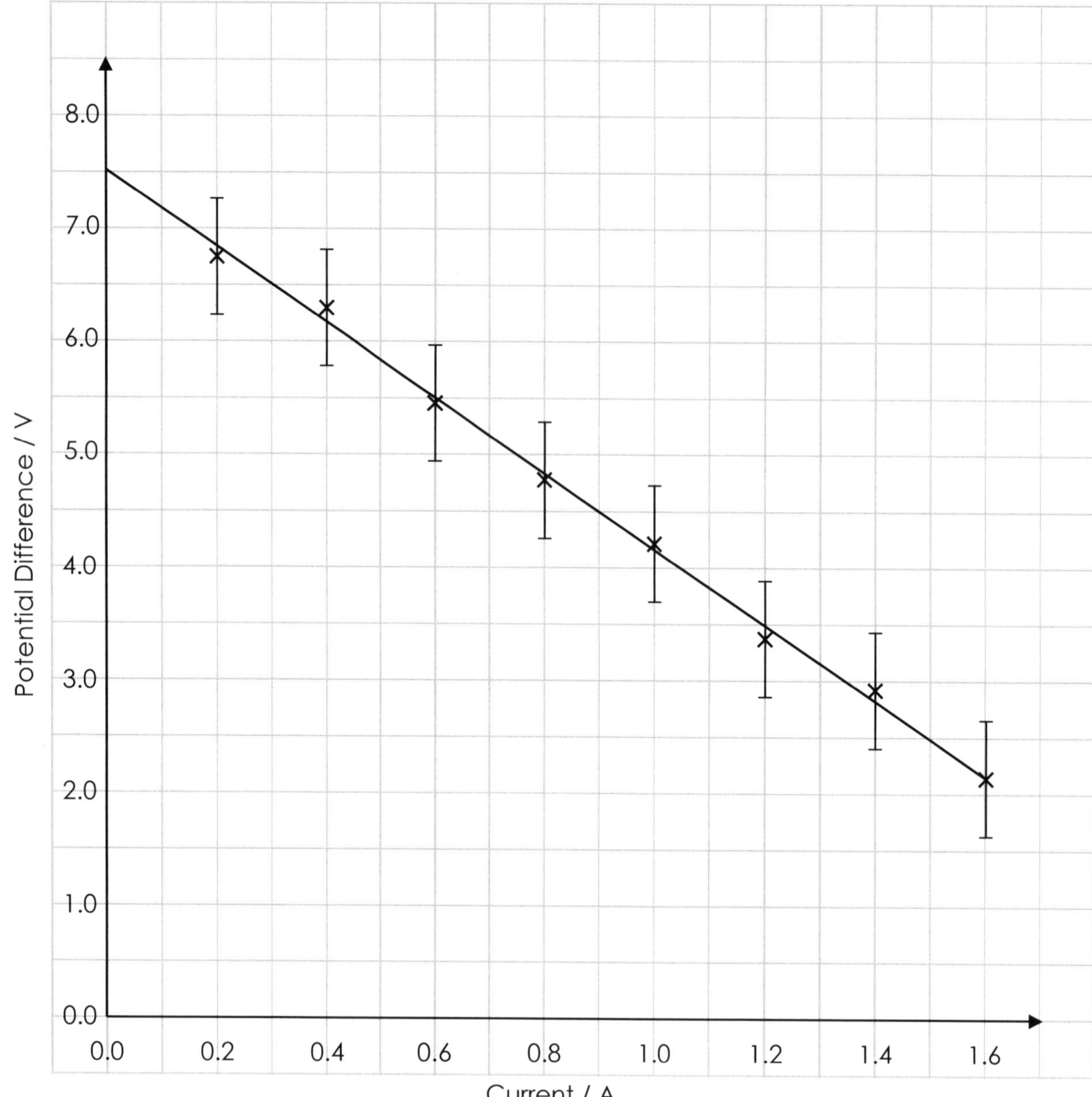

a. Determine the y-intercept of the **line of best fit**

b. Draw in a **worst acceptable** line and determine the **y-intercept** of this line

c. Calculate the **percentage uncertainty** in the y intercept

9th December – Part 2

2. The following data was collected in an A Level practical investigation.

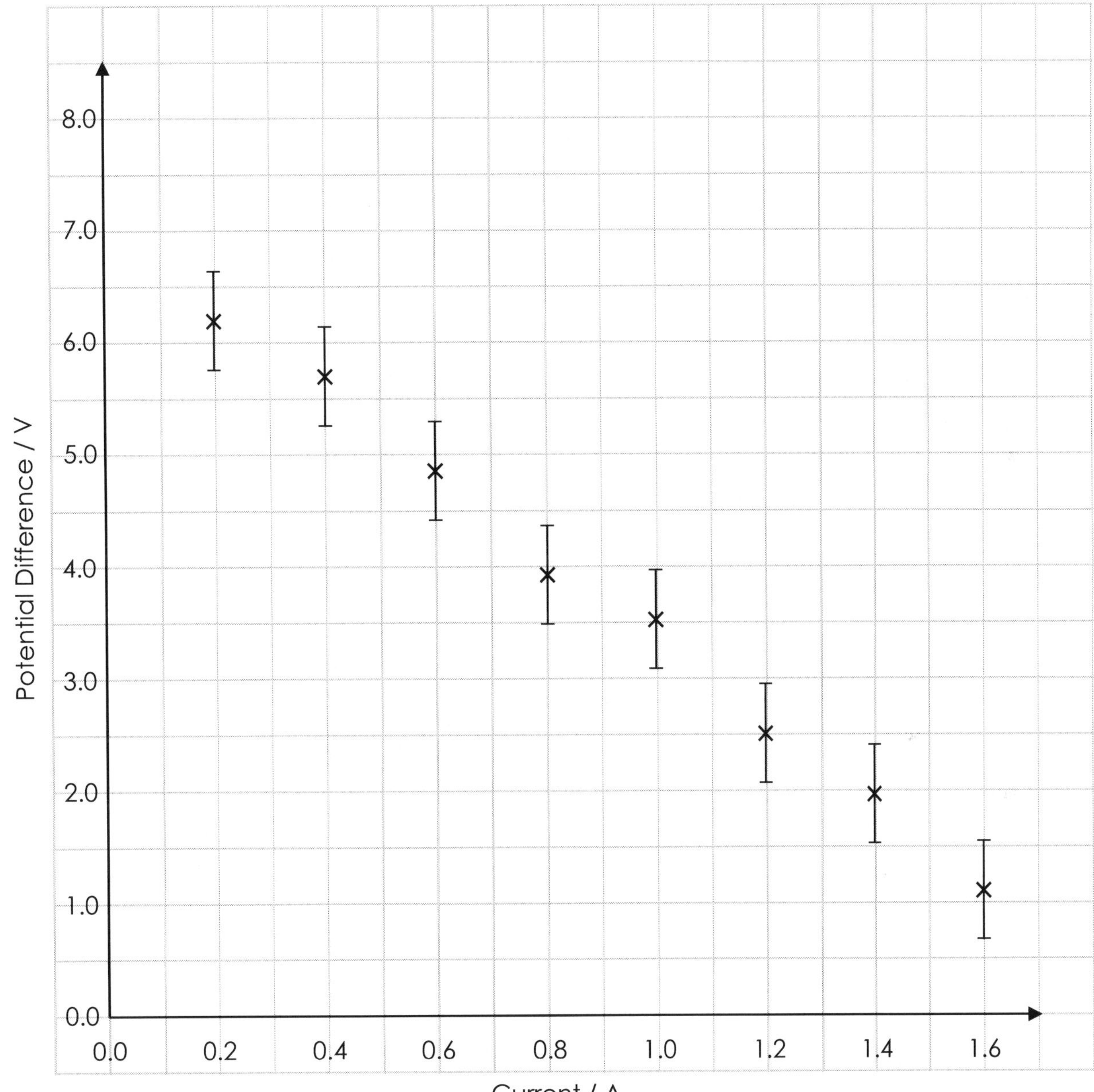

Calculate the **percentage uncertainty** in the **y-intercept**.

10th December

1 2 3

1. **Convert**:

   a. 1.00 eV to kWh

   b. 6.50 TeV to J

2. The following resistors are connected in series.

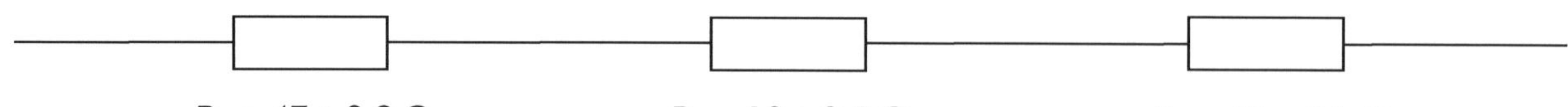

$R_1 = 47 \pm 0.2\ \Omega$ $R_2 = 10 \pm 0.5\ \Omega$ $R_3 = 47 \pm 0.1\ \Omega$

   a. Calculate their **combined** resistance

   b. Calculate the **total uncertainty** in this value

3. A lioness of mass 140 kg is travelling at 22 m s^{-1} when she collides with a stationary baby zebra of mass 45 kg. Following the collision, they move off together.

   Calculate their **speed** following the collision.

11th December

1. An investigation was carried out to calculate the internal resistance of a cell. For the following data, the y-intercept is equal to the EMF. 'E' (sometimes the symbol 'ε' is also used) of the cell and the negative value of the gradient is equal to the internal resistance 'r'.

   Calculate the values of **E** and **r** and the **percentage uncertainty** in the EMF.

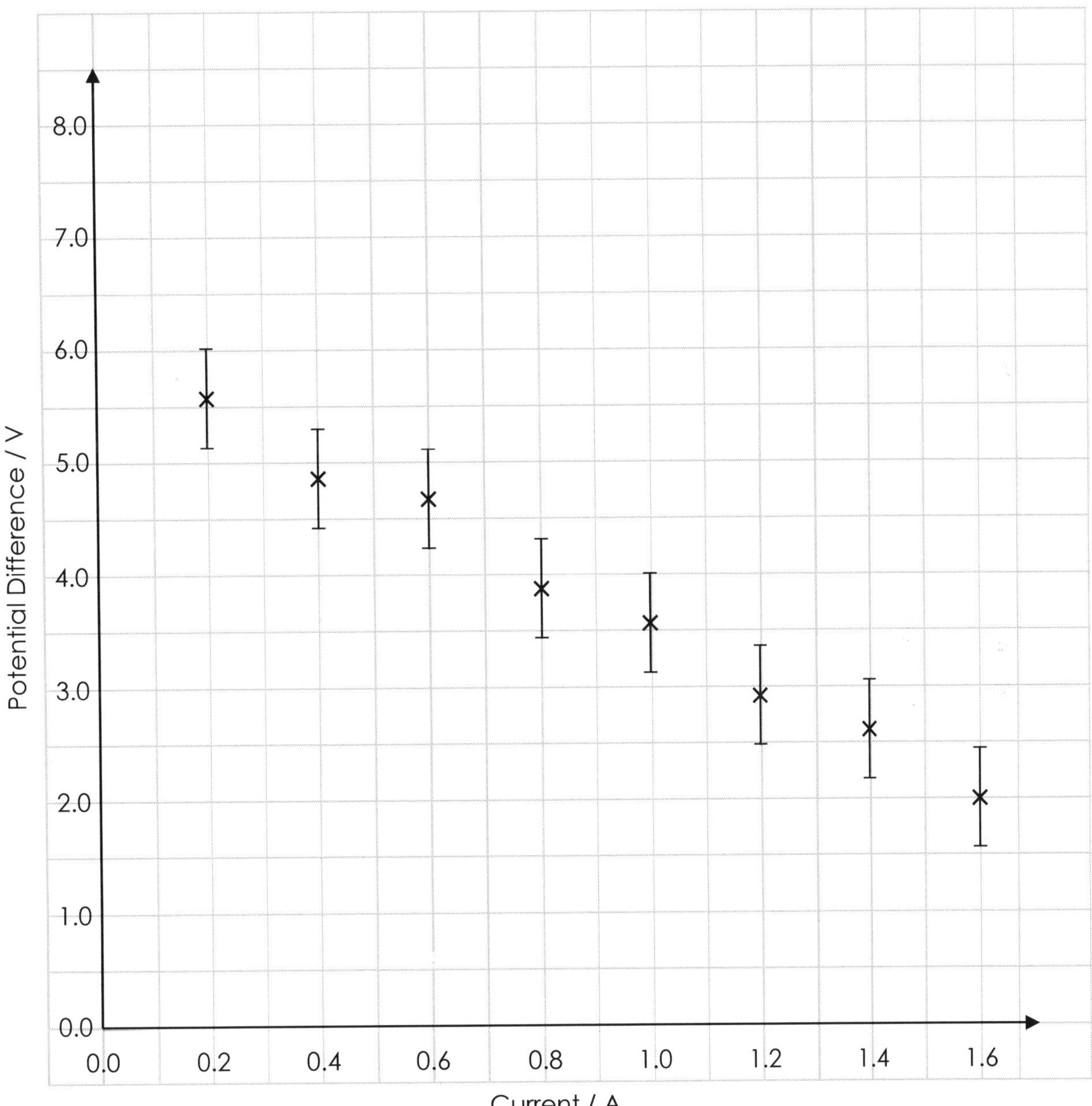

12th December

1 | 2

1. Complete the following **nuclear** equations:

a. $^{239}_{94}Pu \longrightarrow U + \alpha$

b. $^{187}_{75}Re \longrightarrow Os + {}_{-1}\beta$

c. $^{60}_{27}Co \longrightarrow \quad + \gamma$

d. $^{13}_{4}Be \longrightarrow Be + {}_{0}n$

2. Determine the values of **a** and **b** using the gradient and y-intercept.

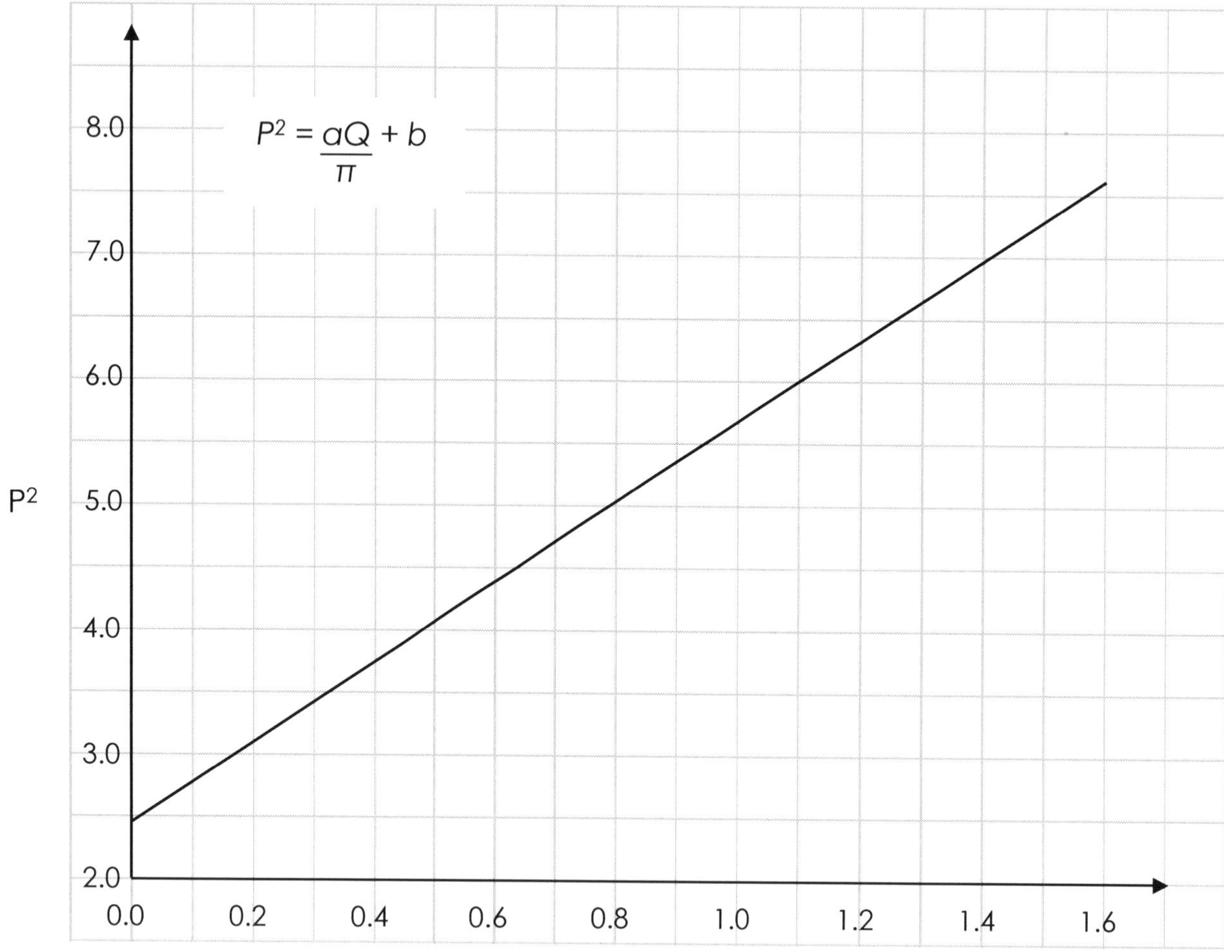

13th December

1 2

1. Sketch a graph showing the **activity** of a radioactive sample against time.

2. Determine the value of the constant **b** and the **percentage uncertainty** in this value.

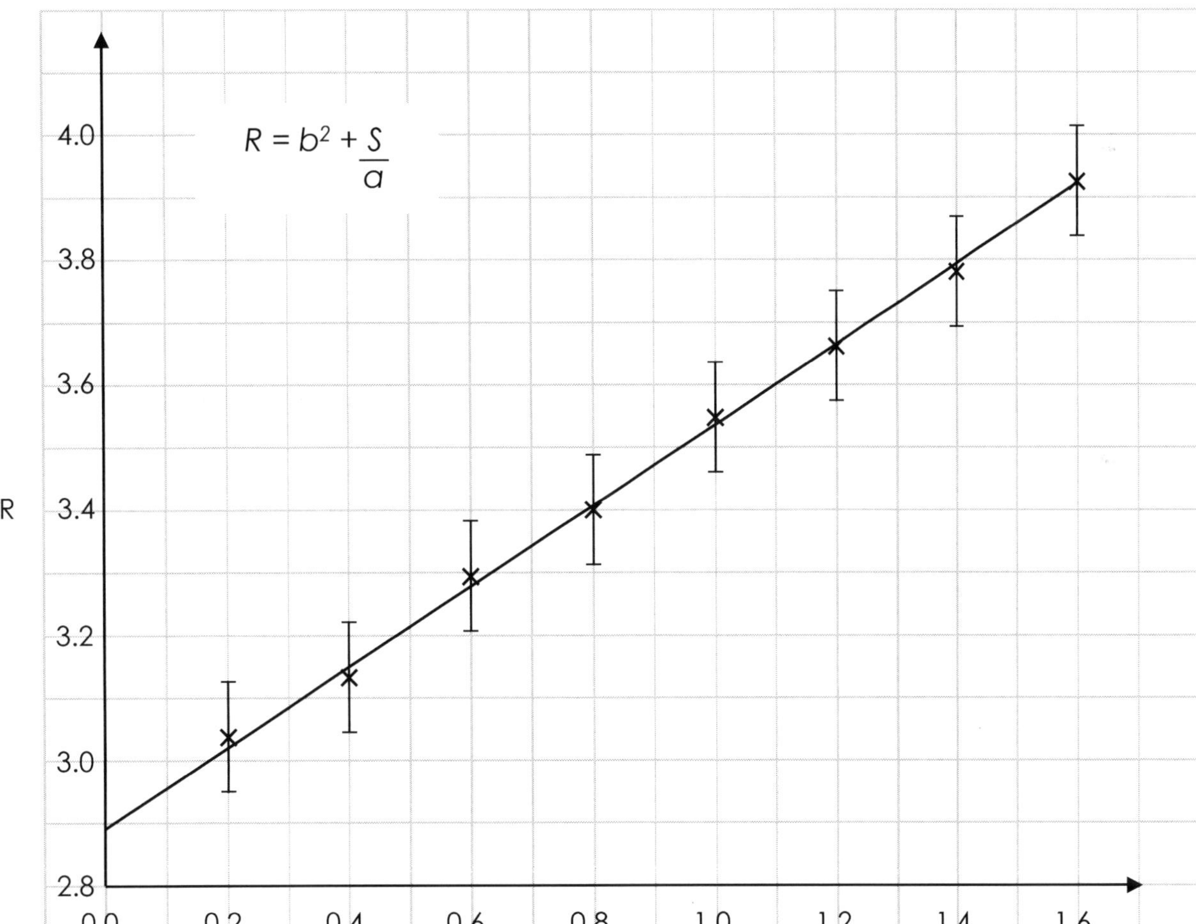

14th December

1 2

1. Sketch a graph showing the **number of nuclei** of a radioactive sample with time.

2. **Complete** the following table:

	Quantity	Symbol	Unit
a.	Acceleration	a	
b.	Capacitance		farad, F
c.	Charge		
d.	Displacement		
e.	Electromotive force		
f.	Gravitational potential		
g.	Gravitational field strength		
h.	Intensity		
i.	Magnetic flux		
j.	Magnetic flux density		
k.	Potential difference		
l.	Pressure		
m.	Radius		
n.	Resistance		
o.	Resistivity		
p.	Specific latent heat		
q.	Strain		
r.	Stress		
s.	Temperature		

15th December

1 2 3

1. Three lamps of resistance 5.0 Ω , 10 Ω and 20 Ω are in parallel with a cell of e.m.f 6.0 V. Calculate the **total current** drawn from the battery. Assume the cell has negligible internal resistance.

2. Calculate the **specific charge** (charge per unit mass) of a proton.

$m_p = 1.67 \times 10^{-27}$ kg and $Q_p = + 1.60 \times 10^{-19}$ C

3. Determine the **amplitude** (in V) and **frequency** of the signal on this oscilloscope trace.

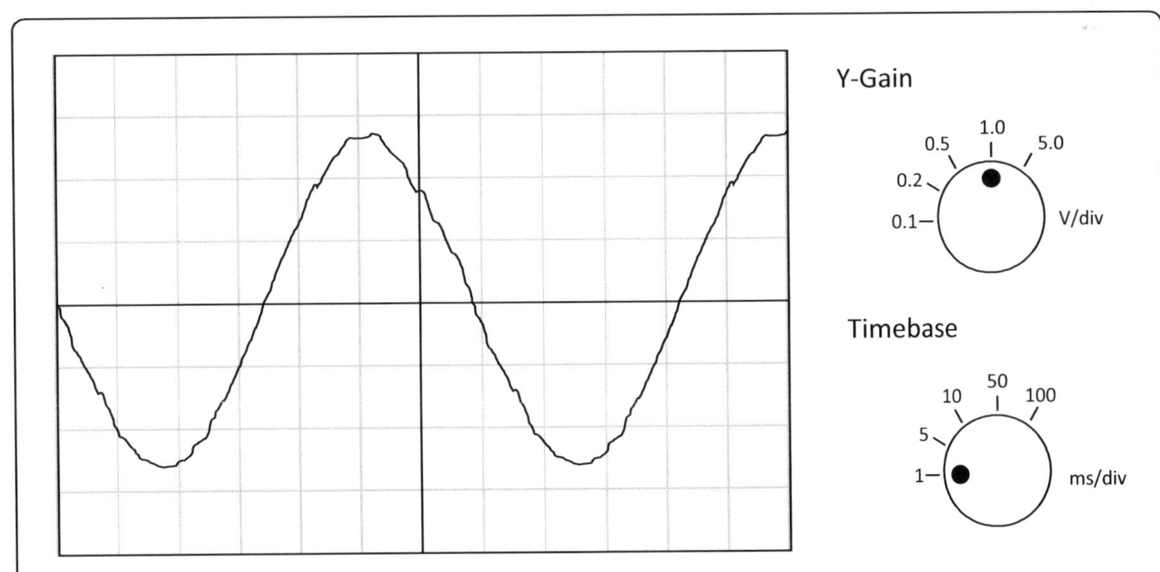

16th December

1 2 3

1. A potential divider consists of a 1.0 kΩ resistor and a 2.0 kΩ resistor. The input potential difference to the potential divider is 6.0 V.

   Calculate the **potential difference** across the 1.0 kΩ resistor.

2. Calculate the **specific charge** of an electron.

   $m_e = 9.11 \times 10^{-31}$ kg and $Q_e = -1.60 \times 10^{-19}$ C

3. Calculate the **internal resistance** of a battery of e.m.f 12 V if its terminal p.d falls to 10 V when it supplies a current of 2.0 A.

17th December

1 2

1. **Sketch** graphs of $y = \cos x$ and $y = \sin x$ on the same axis.

2. **Complete** the following table:

	Quantity	Symbol	Unit
a.	Activity	A	
b.	Amplitude		metre, m
c.	Area		
d.	Critical angle		
e.	Density		
f.	Half-life		
g.	Magnetic flux		
h.	Magnetic flux density		
i.	Period		
j.	Planck's constant		
k.	Refractive index		
l.	Resistance		
m.	Resistivity		
n.	Temperature		
o.	Time		
p.	Time constant		
q.	Wavelength		
r.	Work function		
s.	Young modulus		

18th December

1 2 3

1. Calculate the **specific charge** of a neutron.

m_n = 1.67 x 10^{-27} kg and Q_n = 0 C

2. The volume of a piece of granite is measured by placing it in a measuring cylinder containing water. The level of the water raises from 100 ml to 158 ml. The mass of the rock is 88 g.

   Calculate the **density** of the rock.

3. A battery of negligible internal resistance supplies an e.m.f of 6.0 V to an LDR and a bulb in series with the battery. The LDR has a resistance of 3.0 Ω and the bulb has a resistance of 6.0 Ω.

   Calculate the **potential difference** across the bulb.

19th December

1 2

1. A lamp has a current of 200 mA flowing through it and a resistance of 20 Ω. Calculate the **power** of the lamp.

2. **Complete** the following table:

	Quantity	Symbol	Unit
a.	Angular velocity	ω	
b.	Boltzmann's constant		m^2 kg s^{-2} K^{-1}
c.	Force		
d.	Gravitational constant		
e.	Gravitational field strength		
f.	Gravitational potential		
g.	Gravitational potential energy		
h.	Planck's constant		
i.	Refractive index		
j.	Specific heat capacity		
k.	Specific latent heat		
l.	Speed of light		
m.	Spring constant		
n.	Strain		
o.	Stress		
p.	Weight		
q.	Work done		
r.	Work function		
s.	Young modulus		

20th December

1 2 3

1. A stick is thrown directly upwards in the air and takes 1.80 s to reach its maximum height.

   Calculate the **speed** the stick was thrown at.

2. A gas is stored at a pressure of 480 kPa in an expandable container of initial volume 1.5 m^3.

   Calculate the final **pressure** if the volume slowly increases to 12 m^3 at a constant temperature.

3. A force is applied to a pedal on a mountain bike that is 165 ± 1 mm from the axis of rotation. The torque (moment) is measured with a sensor as 300 Nm ± 2%.

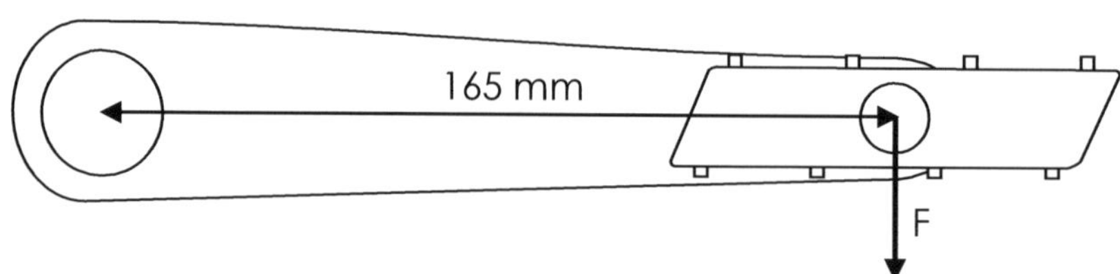

   Calculate the **force** applied and the **total percentage uncertainty** in this value.

21st December

1 2 3

1. A metal wire of original length 1.6 m is extended by 4.1 mm when a force is applied.

   Calculate the **strain** in the wire.

2. A plaster is submerged under 2.00 m of water in the deep end of a swimming pool.

   Calculate the additional **pressure** on this object due to the water above it.

   ρ_{water} = 997 kg m^{-3}

3. The e.m.f of a battery is 4.5 V. When a 10 Ω resistor is connected in series to the battery, the terminal potential difference drops to 4.2 V.

   Calculate the **internal resistance** of the battery.

22nd December

1

1. A piece of SWG* 25 copper wire is 1.00 m long and has a diameter of 0.508 mm.

*Standard Wire Gauge

Quantity	Value
Resistivity	$1.72 \times 10^{-8}\ \Omega$ m
Charge carrier density	8.49×10^{28} m^{-3}
Density	8900 kg m^{-3}
Young modulus	130 GPa
Ultimate tensile strength	210 MPa
Poisson's ratio	0.33
Specific heat capacity	385 J kg^{-1} K^{-1}
Melting point	1083 ˚C
Boiling point	2562 ˚C

Table 1: Data for copper

Use the data in Table 1 to calculate:

a. The **mass** of the wire

b. The **tensile force** that would cause the wire to break

23rd December

1. A piece of SWG 25 copper wire is 1.00 m long and has a diameter of 0.508 mm.

Quantity	Value
Resistivity	$1.72 \times 10^{-8}\ \Omega\ m$
Charge carrier density	$8.49 \times 10^{28}\ m^{-3}$
Density	$8900\ kg\ m^{-3}$
Young modulus	130 GPa
Ultimate tensile strength	210 MPa
Poisson's ratio	0.33
Specific heat capacity	$385\ J\ kg^{-1}\ K^{-1}$
Melting point	1083 ˚C
Boiling point	2562 ˚C

Table 1: Data for copper

Use the data in Table 1, and your previous answers, to calculate:

a. The **resistance** of the wire

b. The **change in temperature** when a current of 250 mA flows for 30 seconds

24th December

1 2

1. Calculate the **relative mass** of an electron if its mass is 9.11×10^{-31} kg and a proton's mass is 1.67×10^{-27} kg, providing that the relative mass of a proton is exactly 1.

2. Describe, with the aid of a labelled diagram, Sir Joseph John Thomson's **plum pudding** model of the atom.

25th December

1 2

1. A free neutron undergoes beta minus decay with a half-life of just over 10 minutes. Write an **equation** describing this process.

2. Briefly describe, with the aid of a diagram, Ernest Rutherford's **nuclear** model of the atom and the experiments carried out by Hans Geiger and Ernest Marsden.

26th December

1. A piece of SWG 25 copper wire is 1.00 m long and has a diameter of 0.508 mm.

Quantity	Value
Resistivity	$1.72 \times 10^{-8}\ \Omega$ m
Charge carrier density	8.49×10^{28} m^{-3}
Density	8900 kg m^{-3}
Young modulus	130 GPa
Ultimate tensile strength	210 MPa
Poisson's ratio	0.33
Specific heat capacity	385 J kg^{-1} K^{-1}
Melting point	1083 ˚C
Boiling point	2562 ˚C

Table 1: Data for copper

Use the data in Table 1, and your previous answers, to calculate:

a. The **extension** when a 100 N tensile load is applied

b. The **electron drift velocity** when a p.d. of 1.50 V is applied across the ends of the wire*

*This is not covered in the AQA spec

27th December

1

1. The following procedure is used to find the value of the resistance R_5.

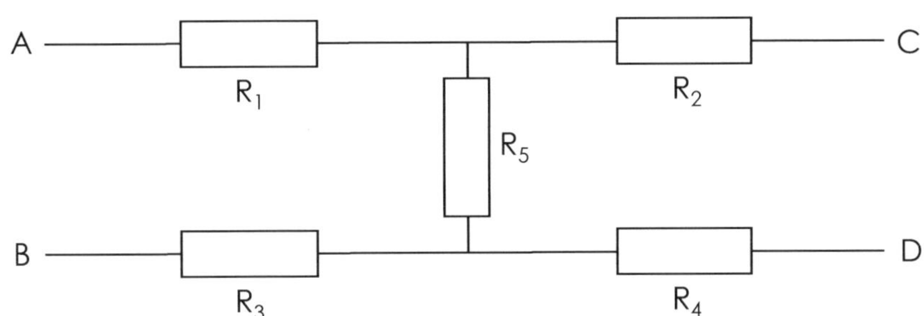

A potential difference of 1.5 V is connected in turn across various points in the arrangement.

- With 1.5 V applied across terminals AC a current of 37.5 mA flows
- With 1.5 V applied across terminals BD a current of 25 mA flows
- With 1.5 V applied across terminals AB a current of 30 mA flows
- With 1.5 V applied across terminals CD a current of 15 mA flows

a. Write down three **equations** for the total resistance between BD, AB and CD in terms of R_1, R_2, R_3, R_4 and R_5

$R_{AC} = R_1 + R_2$ $\qquad$ $R_{BD} =$

$R_{AB} =$ $\qquad$ $R_{CD} =$

b. Calculate the **resistance** between AC, BD, AB and CD

$R_{AC} =$ $\qquad$ $R_{BD} =$

$R_{AB} =$ $\qquad$ $R_{CD} =$

c. Determine the **value** of resistor R_5

Adapted from a BPhO question from the 2010 Year 12 Challenge

28th December

1 2 3

1. Calculate the **specific charge** of a helium nucleus.

$m_{He} = 6.646 \times 10^{-27}$ kg

2. Five measurements of the diameter of a wire are made: 1.10 mm, 1.05 mm, 1.02 mm, 1.11 mm and 1.12 mm.

   Calculate the **mean** diameter and its **absolute certainty**.

3. An F-35B Lightning jet flies at Mach 1.5 (510 m s^{-1}) on a bearing of 034°.

   Draw a sketch diagram and calculate the **components** of velocity in the northerly and easterly directions.

29th December

1 2 3

1. Calculate the **activity** of a sample, that had an original activity of 1000 Bq, after 3 half-lives.

2. A tennis ball is hit at an initial velocity of 20.5 m s^{-1} at an angle of 10.0 degrees above the horizontal.

   Calculate the **horizontal** and **vertical** components of the tennis ball's velocity.

3. Each identical resistor in the network has a resistance of R.

   Calculate the **combined resistance** between A and B in terms of R.

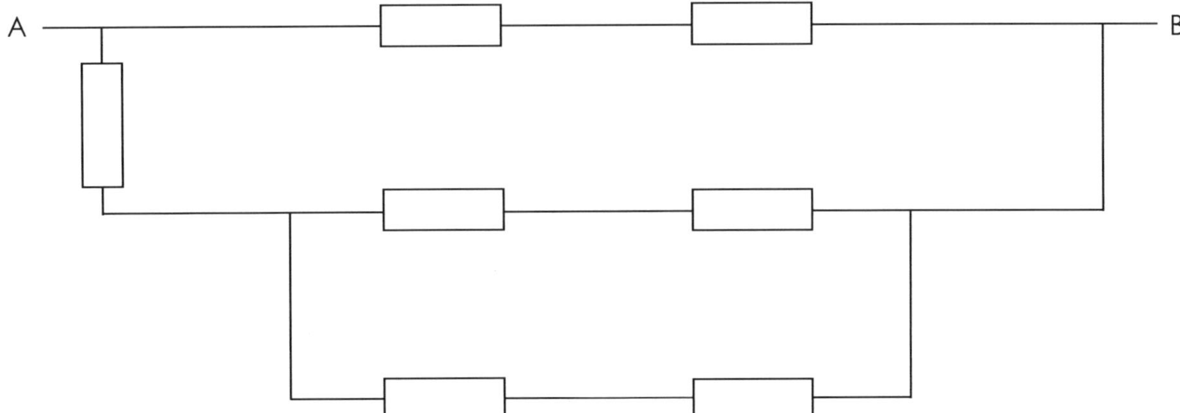

30th December

1 | 2

1. Write down the following **values** (from memory if possible):

    a. Mass of an electron

    b. Mass of a neutron

    c. Charge of a proton

    d. One electronvolt in joules

    e. Wavelength of red light

2. Each identical resistor in the network has a resistance of R.

    Calculate the **combined resistance** between A and B in terms of R.

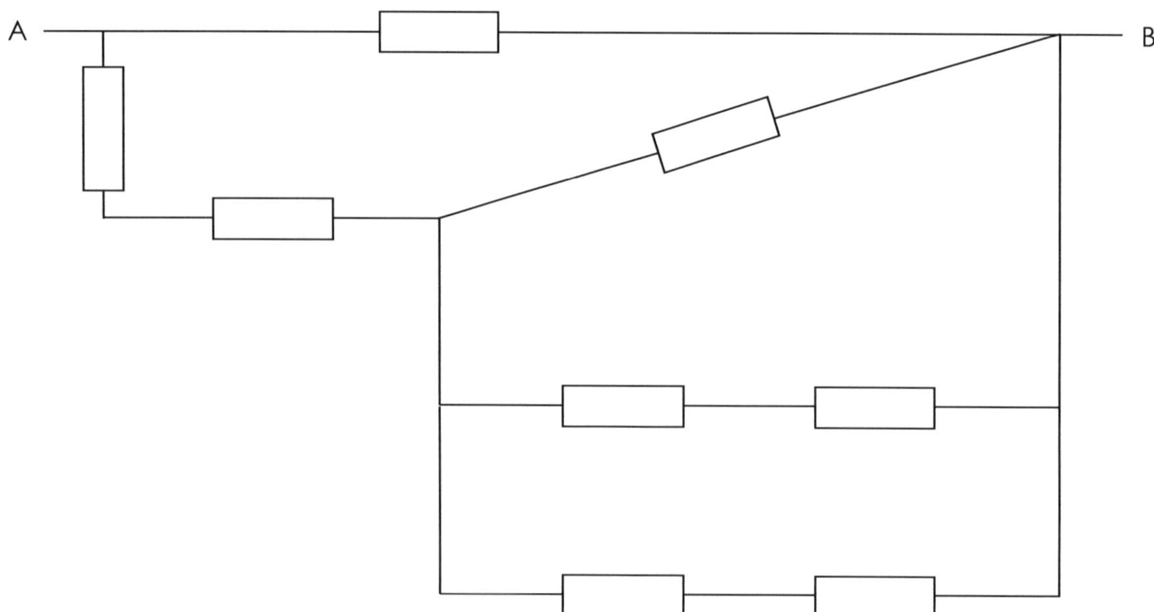

31st December

1. Using the graph below:

    a. Calculate the **maximum positive acceleration**

    b. Estimate the **displacement** between 3.5 s and 8.0 s

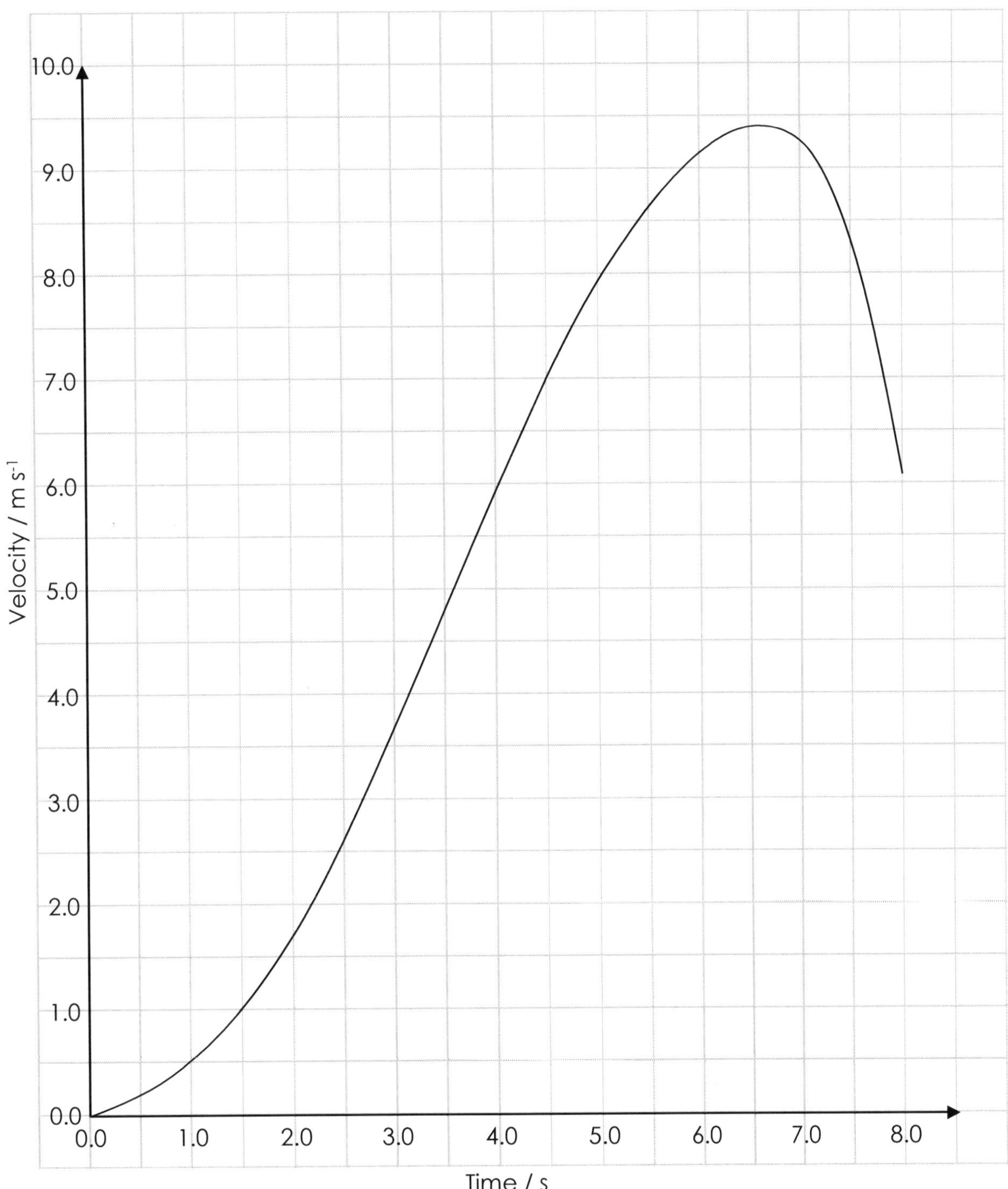

DECEMBER REVIEW

Just like in November, reflect on the progress you have made and have another go at any questions you may have missed this last month.

A Level Physics Content	Red	Amber	Green
I can **convert** between different units for measuring energy.			
I can draw a **worst acceptable** line of best fit.			
I can calculate the percentage uncertainty in a **line of best fit**.			
I can calculate the percentage uncertainty in a **y-intercept**.			
I can recall **units** of common quantities.			
I can calculate the **combined resistance** of resistor combinations.			

Any other comments:

JANUARY

JANUARY

The New Year is often a period of time when you take time to reflect, look forward and consider the small changes you can make to improve certain aspects of your life.

The changes you are most likely to stick to are ones that are not too drastic. If some of these small resolutions can become habits, their effects will compound over time leading to large improvements.

That is why you're working through this workbook now. A small amount of work every day will have a big impact months down the line.

1st January

1 2 3

1. Write down some **small goals** you have for the end of this academic year.

   a.

   b.

   c.

2. Write down some **small changes** you can realistically make to work towards these goals.

3. Spend a **few minutes** looking back through the work in this book (and The Daily Workout Book 1) to see the quantity of work you have already completed. You have already achieved a lot!

2nd January

1 2 3

1. Write down the **value** and **units** for the following constants:

   a. Gravitational field strength on Earth

   b. Gravitational constant

   c. Planck's constant

2. Define:

   a. **Phase** difference

   b. **Path** difference

3. The diagram below shows a wave diffracting through an aperture (gap) that is approximately the **same size** as the wavelength.

   Using a **pencil** and **compass**, add **3** more **wavefronts** to the diagram.

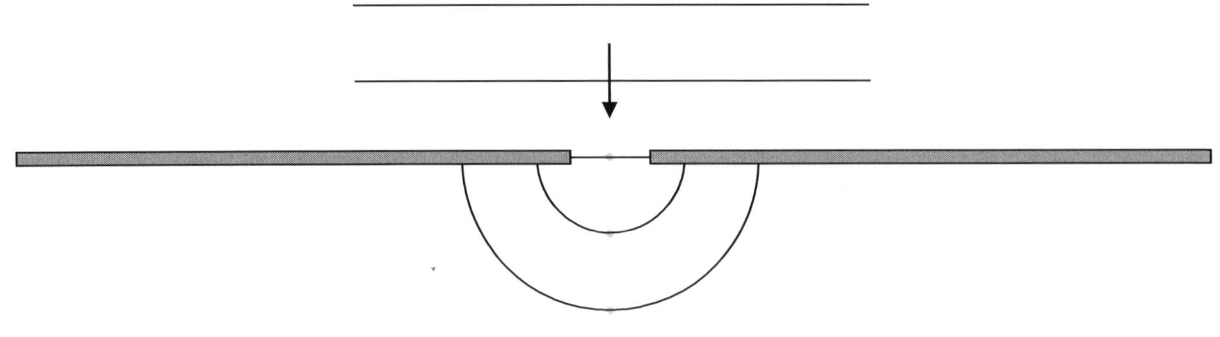

3rd January

1 2 3

1. Write down the **value** and **units** for the following constants:

   a. Planck's constant

   b. Boltzmann constant

   c. Molar gas constant

2. Define:

   a. **Node**

   b. **Antinode**

3. The diagram below shows a wave diffracting through an aperture that is much **larger** than the wavelength.

   Using a **pencil** and **compass**, add **3** more **wavefronts** to the diagram.

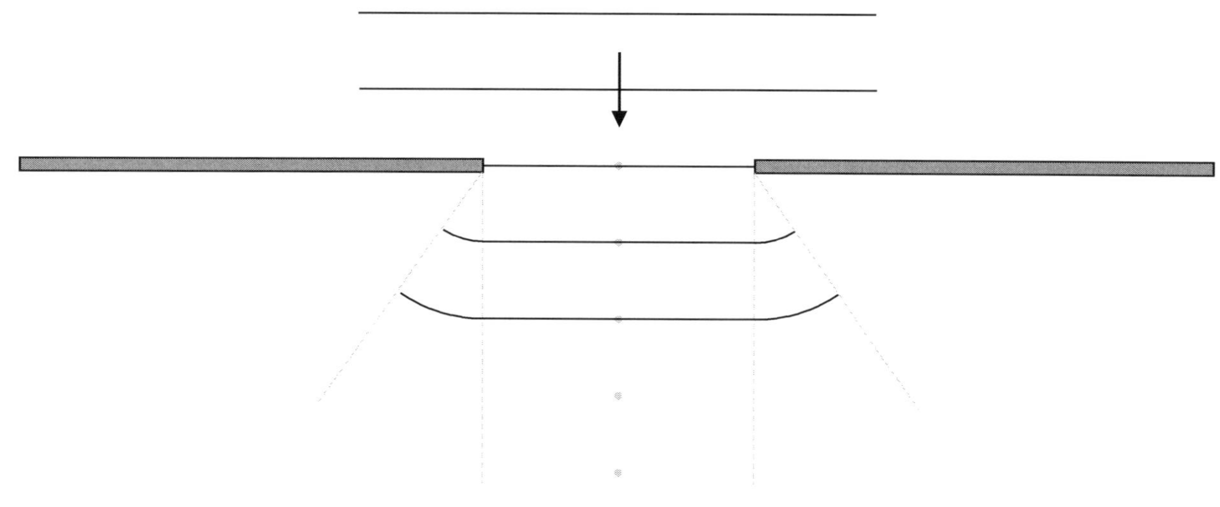

4th January

1 2 3

1. Water has a specific heat capacity of 4182 J kg^{-1} °C^{-1}. Calculate the **energy** it takes to heat 568 ml of water from an initial temperature of 22 °C to a final temperature of 60 °C.

ρ_{Water} = 997 kg m^{-3}

2. A Napoleonic cannon of mass 1200 kg is initially at rest. It fires a twelve-pound cannonball of mass 5.44 kg at a horizontal velocity of +439 m s^{-1}. Calculate the initial **recoil velocity** of the cannon.

3. The diagram below shows a wave diffracting past the **edge** of an obstacle.

   Using a **pencil** and **compass**, add **3** more **wavefronts** to the diagram.

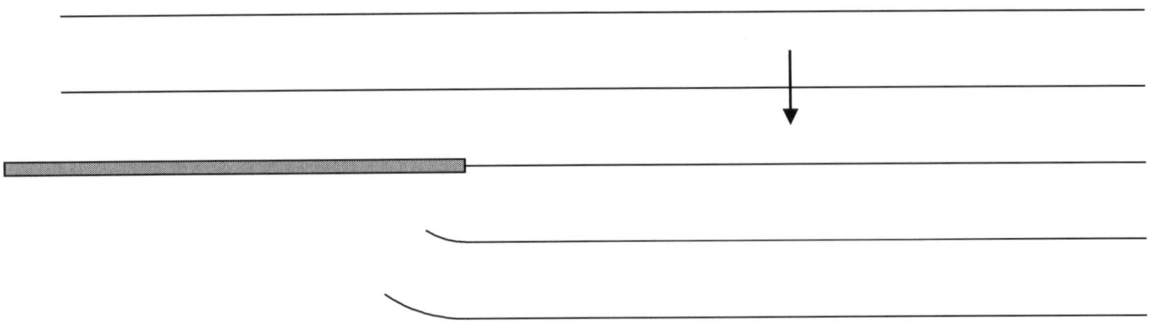

5th January

1 2 3

1. Ultrasound travels at a speed of 330 m s^{-1} in air and 1580 m s^{-1} in skin. Calculate the **change in wavelength** as a 20 MHz wave passes from one medium to the other.

2. Define:

   a. **Electromotive force**

   b. **Potential difference**

3. Complete the diagram showing **3** more **wavefronts** as the wave passes through **two adjacent** slits.

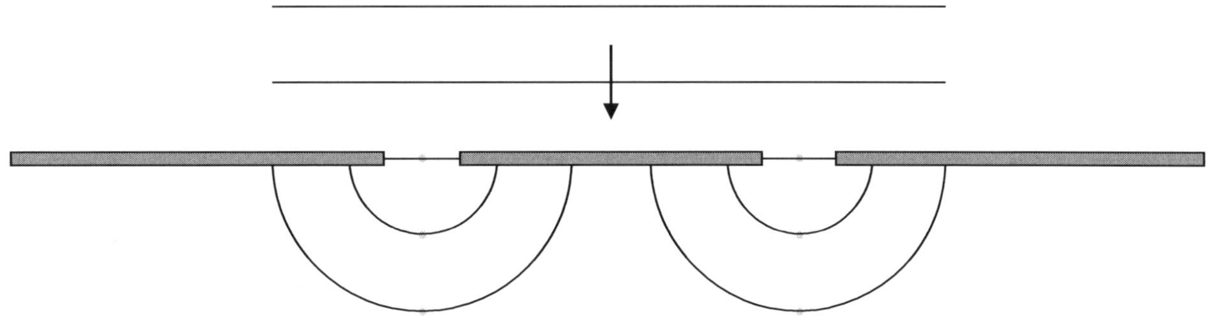

6th January

1. This diagram shows a wave that diffracts through two adjacent slits. The darker thicker line represents a wave peak and the lighter thinner line represents the trough.

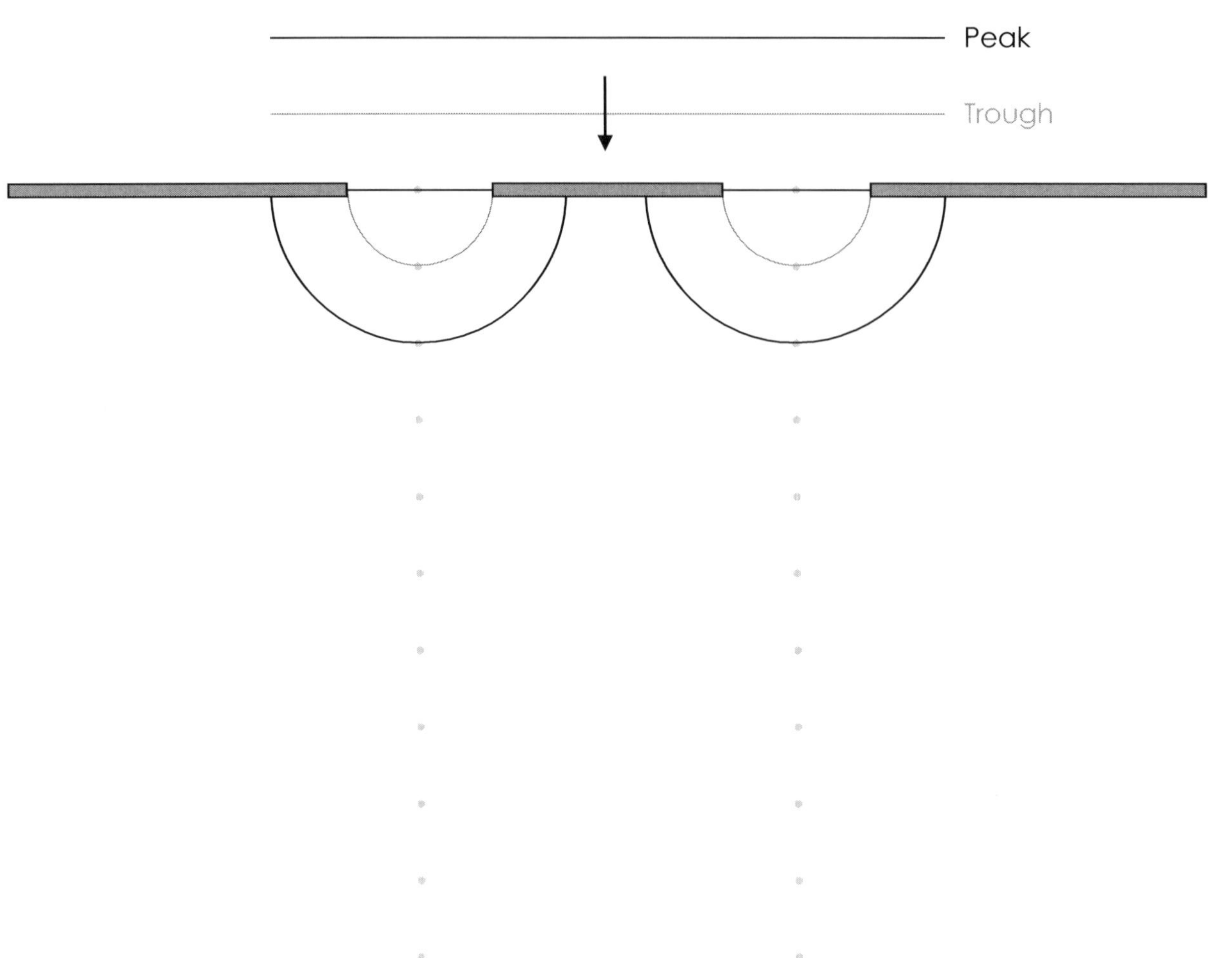

a. Add **4** darker lines and **4** lighter lines to each set of diffracted waves

b. Add crosses to your diagram where a **peak** meets a **peak**

c. Add crosses to your diagram where a **trough** meets a **trough**

7th January

1. This diagram shows a wave that diffracts through two adjacent slits, slightly further apart than yesterday. As before, the darker thicker line represents a wave peak and the lighter thinner line represents the trough.

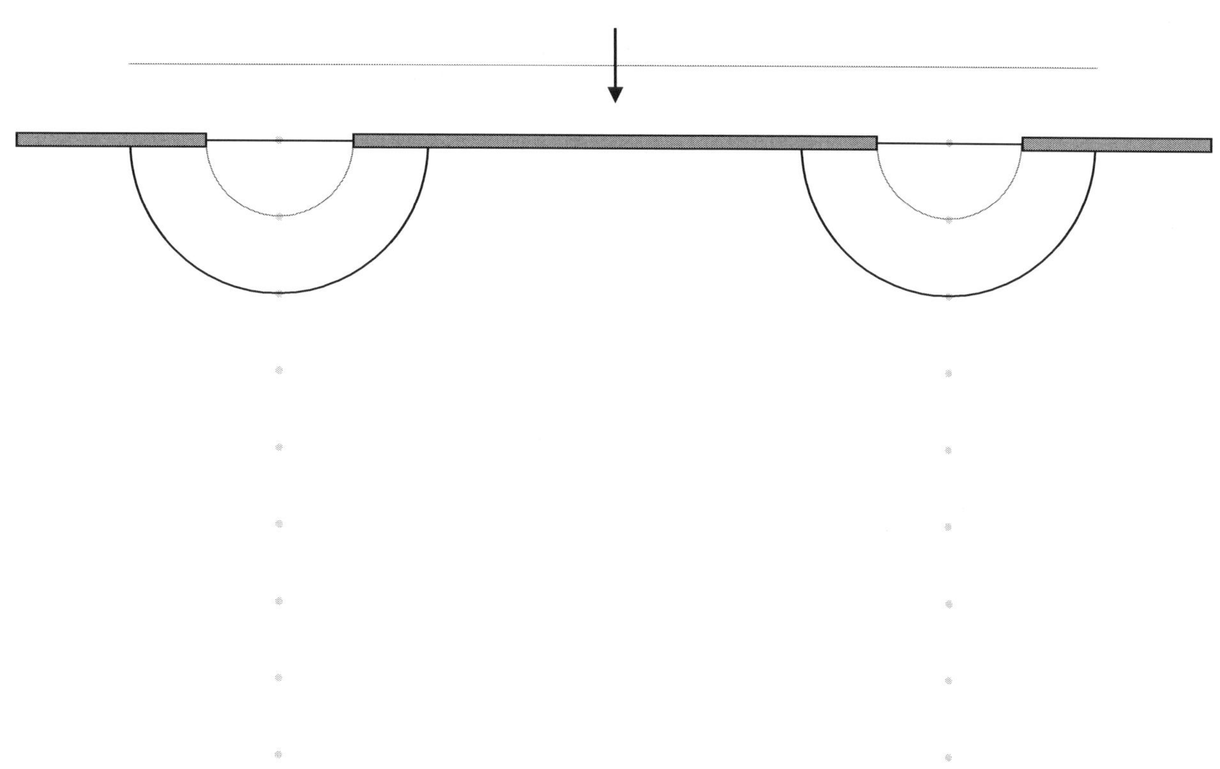

   a. Add **4** darker lines and **4** lighter lines to each set of diffracted waves
   b. Add crosses to your diagram where a **peak** meets a **peak**
   c. Add crosses to your diagram where a **trough** meets a **trough**
   d. **Compare** this pattern to the pattern when the slits were closer together

8th January

1 2 3

1. Write down the **value** and **units** for the following constants:

   a. Elementary charge

   b. Wien's constant

   c. Proton rest mass

2. A green laser of wavelength 532 nm is incident on a double slit with a separation of 0.020 mm. The interference pattern is viewed on a screen at a distance of 2.5 m away from the double slit.

   Calculate the **fringe spacing**.

3. A uniform (i.e. the mass acts at the centre) 104 g metre ruler is supported at each end by triangular pieces of metal. A 300 g mass is supported with the centre of mass exactly 14.2 cm from end A.

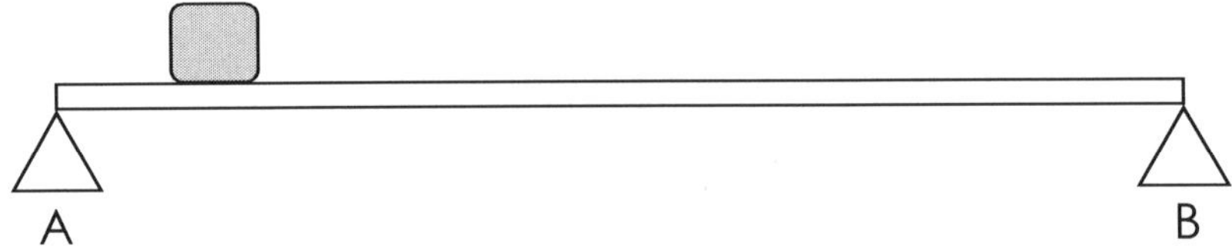

   a. Calculate the total **clockwise** moment about the point A

   b. Calculate the **force** provided by support B

9th January

1 2 3

1. Write down the **value** and **units** for the following constants:

   a. Boltzmann constant

   b. Stefan's constant

   c. Avogadro's number

2. Describe how a **stationary** wave on a guitar string is formed.

3. A uniform 104 g metre ruler is supported by triangular pieces of metal A and B at 11.0 cm and 35.0 cm from each end respectively. A 400 g mass is supported with the centre of mass exactly 18.2 cm from point A.

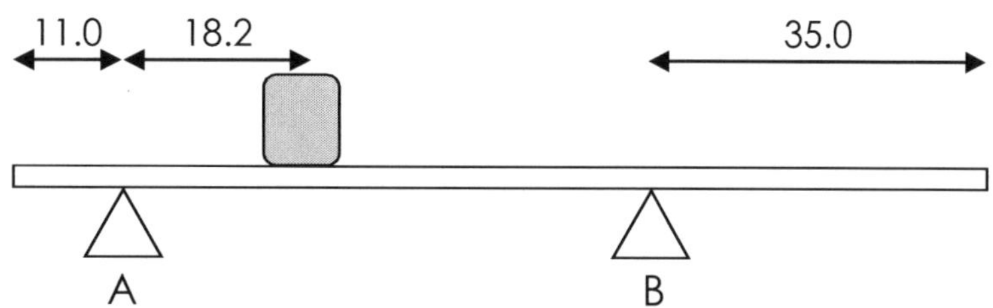

   a. Calculate the total **clockwise** moment about A

   b. Calculate the **force** provided by support B

10th January

1 2 3

1. Write down the **value** and **units** for the following constants:

   a. Gravitational constant

   b. Boltzmann constant

   c. Permittivity of free space

2. A practical is carried out to investigate the frequency of stationary waves. A string of length 1.50 m and mass per unit length of 0.020 kg m^{-1} has a tension of 25.0 N in it.

   Calculate the **frequency** of the **first** harmonic.

3. A spring is stretched and the data plotted on the graph below.

   a. Calculate the **spring constant**

   b. Calculate the **elastic potential energy** stored in the spring when extended by 55 mm

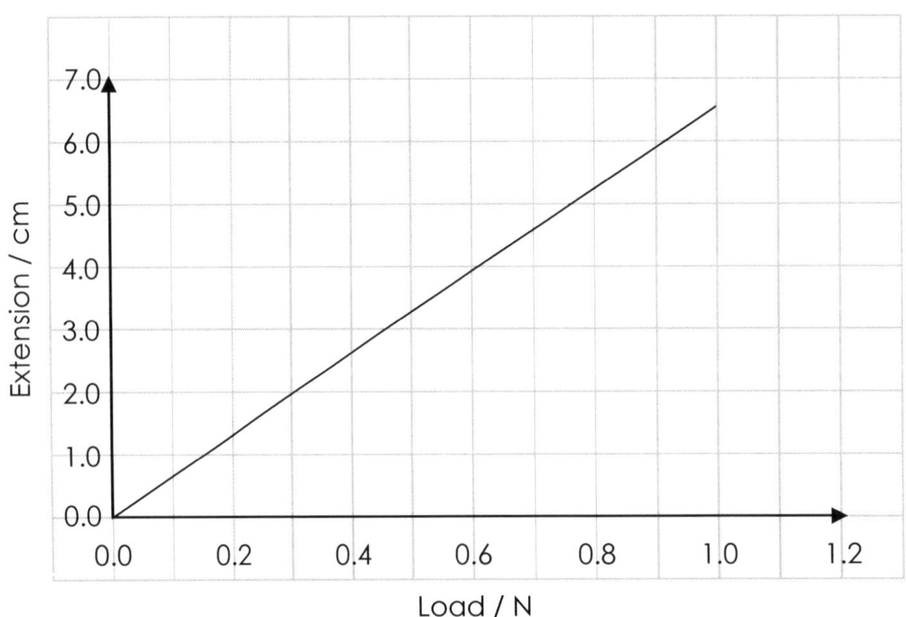

11th January

1 2 3

1. A radio controlled car has a kinetic energy of 40.4 J and is travelling at a velocity of 6.7 m s^{-1}. It hits an obstacle and loses 80 % of its kinetic energy. Calculate the **velocity** of the car after the collision.

2. A 424 g football is accidentally kicked horizontally off a cliff of height 25.0 m at a speed of 8.0 m s^{-1}. Calculate how far the ball travels **horizontally** before it reaches the bottom of the cliff.

3. A spring is stretched and the data plotted on the graph below.

   a. Calculate the **spring constant**

   b. Calculate the elastic **potential energy** stored in the spring when extended by 20 mm

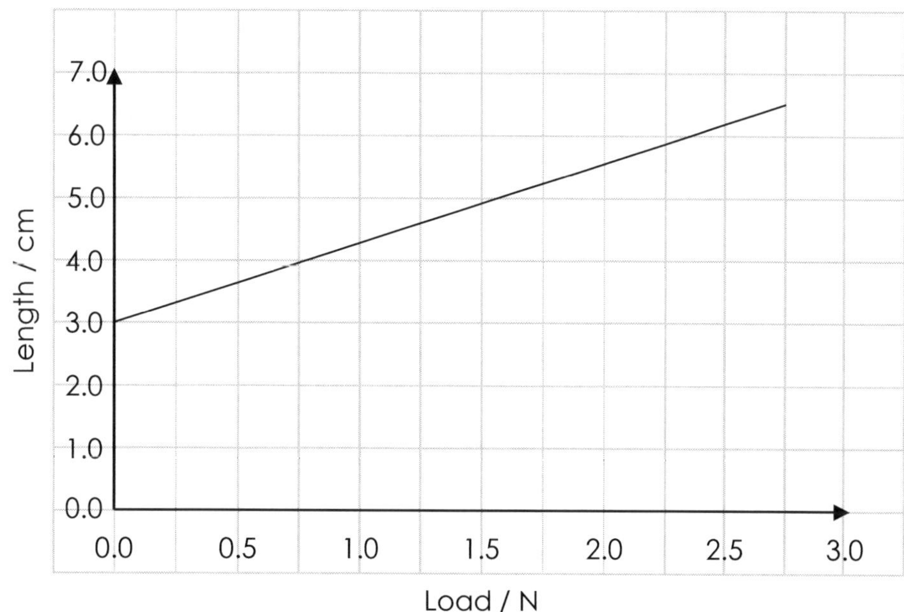

12th January

1 2 3

1. Write down the **value** and **units** for the following constants:

   a. Planck's constant

   b. Permittivity of free space

   c. Speed of EM waves in a vacuum

2. Define:

   a. **Resistance**

   b. **Internal resistance**

3. A uniform 104 g metre ruler is supported by triangular pieces of metal and supports two masses of 400 g and 800 g as shown below.

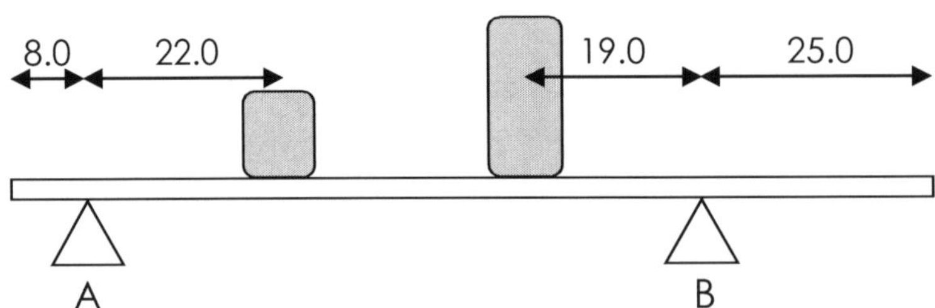

   a. Calculate the **force** provided by support A

   b. Calculate the **force** provided by support B

13th January

1 2 3

1. A ray of light hits a mirror at an angle of 29 degrees to the surface of the mirror. Calculate the **angle of reflection**.

2. Measurements were made to determine the diameter and length of a wire.

Quantity	Percentage Uncertainty
Diameter	2.8 %
Length	0.4 %

Calculate the **percentage uncertainty** in the calculated value of **volume**.

3. A string of length 60 cm is vibrating in its second harmonic. A signal generator vibrates one end of the string at a frequency of 60 Hz and there is a tension of 0.20 N in the string. Calculate the **mass per unit length** of the string.

14th January

1. The following data, as defined by the ISO 216 standard, is for A series paper.

Size	Width / mm	Height / mm	Area / m^2
A4	210	297	
A3	297	420	
A2	420	594	
A1	594	841	
A0	841	1189	

a. Calculate the **area**, in m^2, for each size of paper

b. Plot the data on the **graph** on the next page

c. Calculate the **gradient** to 3 s.f.

d. Express the **ratio** of the height to the width as a surd

e. B series paper has the same aspect ratio (height to width) as the A series. B2 paper is often used for posters and is 500 mm wide. Calculate the **height** of the paper.

14th January

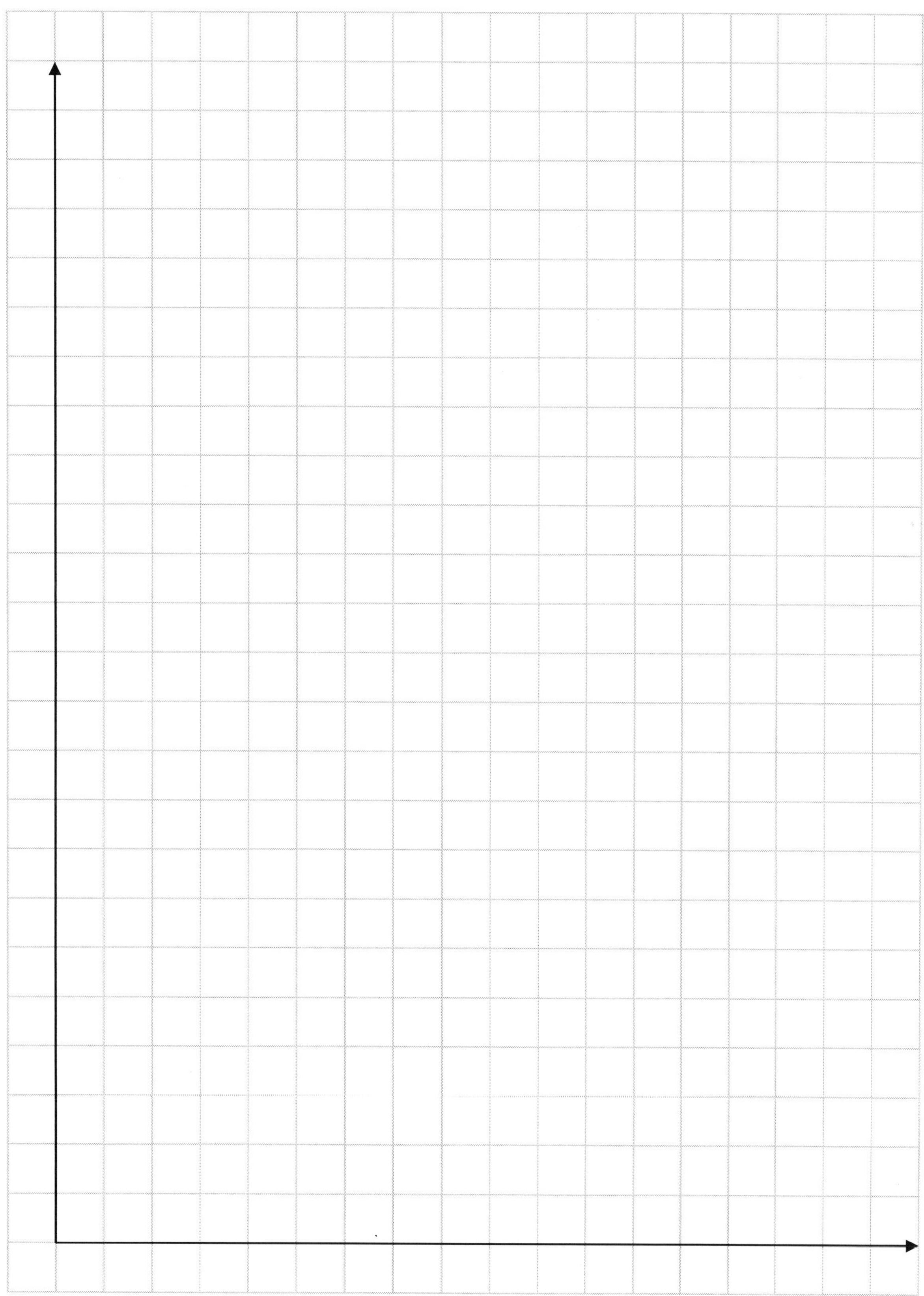

15th January

1 2

1. A ray of light hits a curved mirror that has a radius of 8.0 cm and reflects such that the angle between the incident ray and the reflected ray is 80 degrees. Calculate the **angle of reflection**.

2. **Complete** the following table:

	Quantity	Symbol	Unit
a.	Area		
b.	Magnetic flux density		
c.	Capacitance		
d.	Diameter		
e.	Electromotive force		
f.	Force		
g.	Gravitational constant		
h.	Planck's constant		
i.	Current		
j.	Jerk		
k.	Boltzmann constant		
l.	Length		
m.	Mass		
n.	Refractive index		
o.	Stress		
p.	Momentum		
q.	Charge		
r.	Radius		
s.	Displacement		

16th January

1 2 3

1. Calculate the cross-sectional **area**, in m^2, of the following wires (diameter given in mm):
   a. SWG 7/0 (12.700)
   b. SWG 25 (0.508)
   c. SWG 30 (0.315)
   d. SWG 50 (0.025)

2. Read the **quantity** measured in the following diagrams of vernier scales.

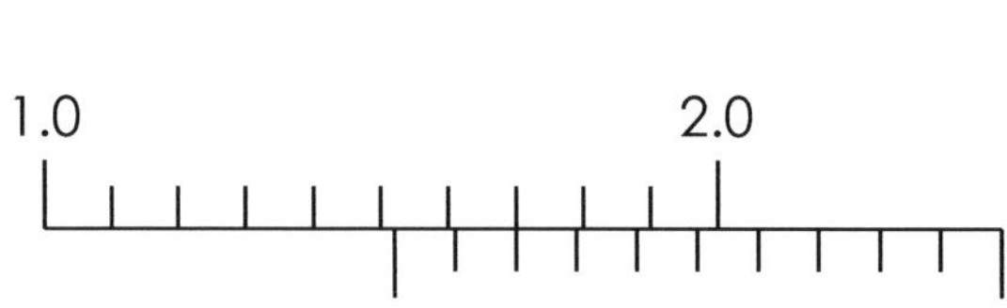

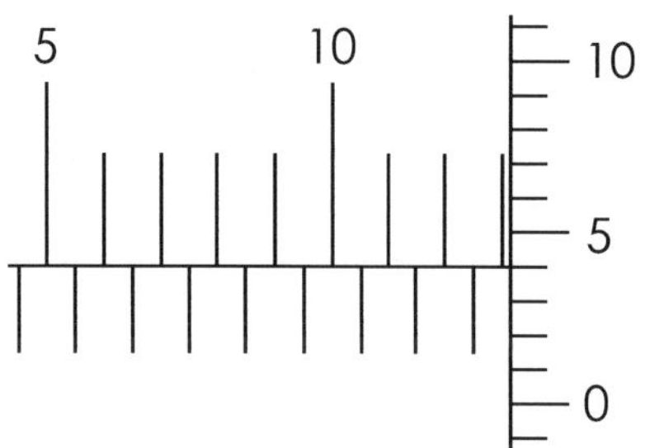

3. Calculate the **refractive index** of the semi-circular block.

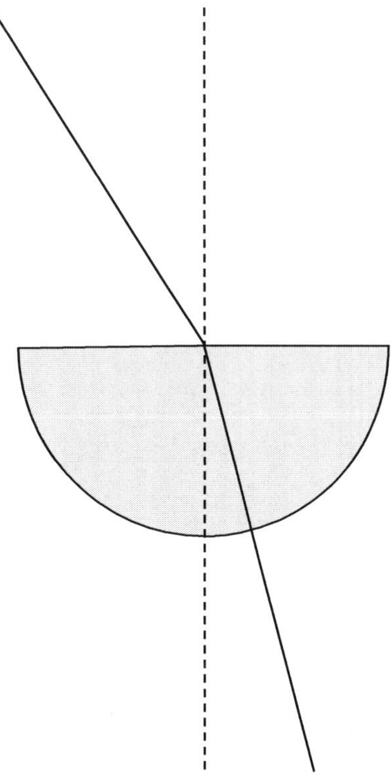

17th January

1 2 3

1. Light enters a glass block of refractive index 1.3 at an angle of 40° to the normal. Calculate the angle of **refraction**.

2. Read the **quantity** measured in the following diagrams of vernier scales.

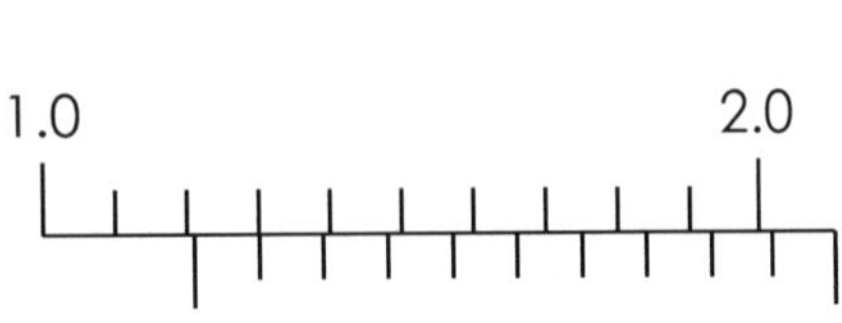

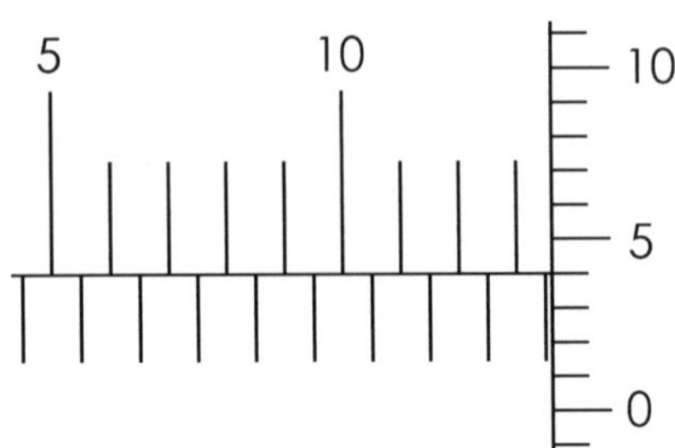

3. Calculate the total **impulse** (change in momentum) from the graph below.

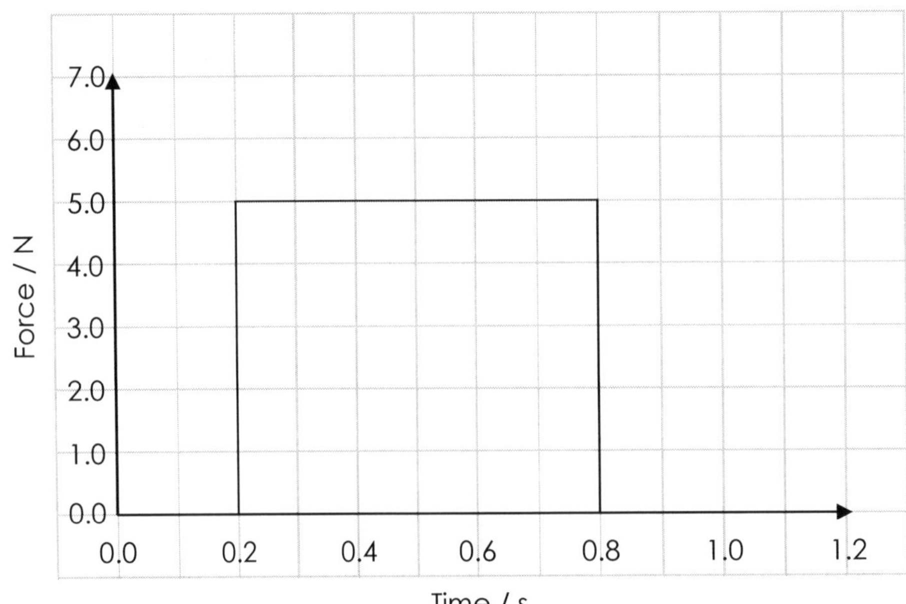

18th January

1 2 3

1. Calculate the **force** needed to accelerate a 630 kg bobsleigh at 2G.

2. Read the **quantity** measured in the following diagrams of vernier scales.

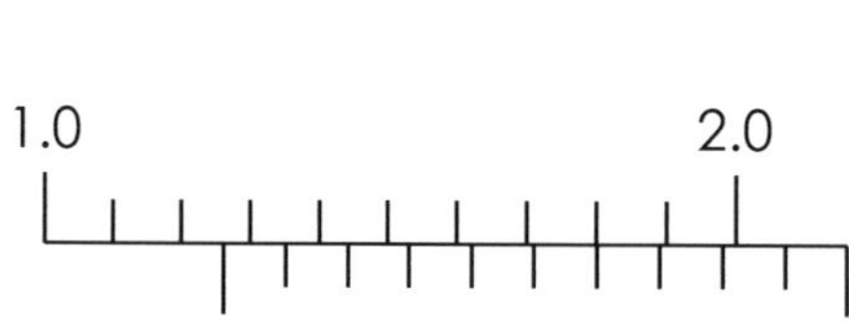

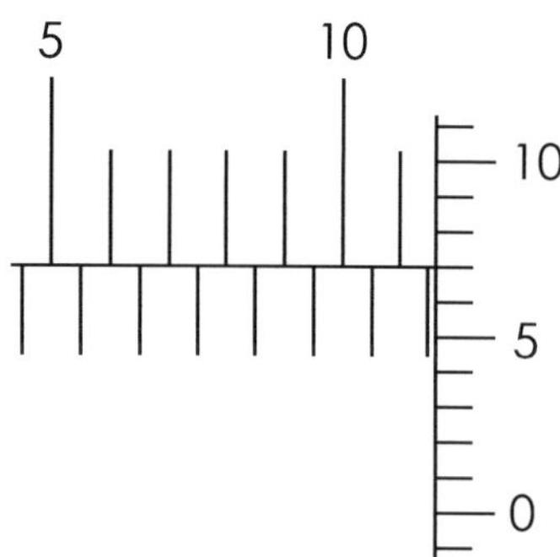

3. Calculate the total **impulse** (change in momentum) from the graph below.

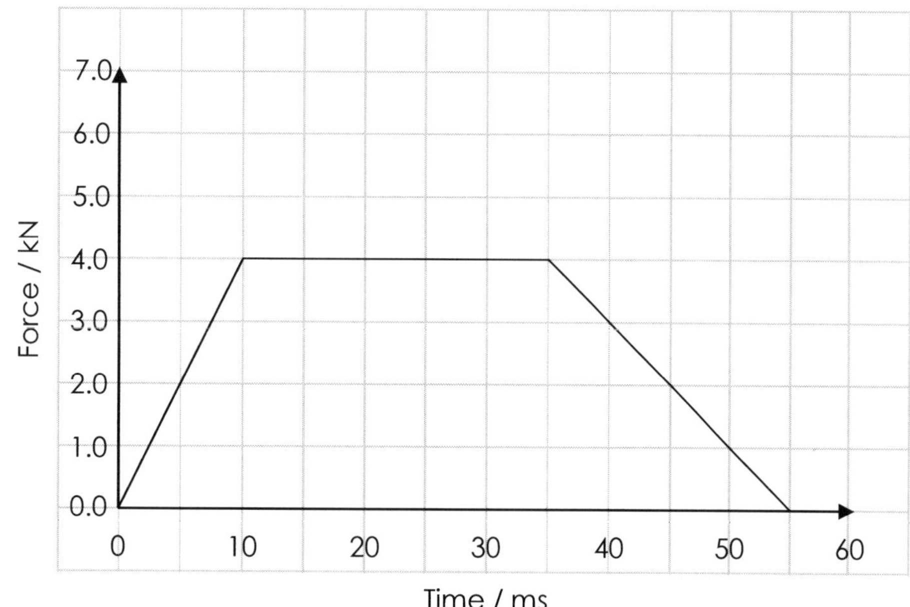

19th January

1 2 3

1. Rearrange the following to make **M** the subject:
   a. $V_g = -GM / r$
   b. $g = -GM / r^2$
   c. $F = -GMm / r^2$

2. Read the **quantity** measured in the following diagrams of vernier scales.

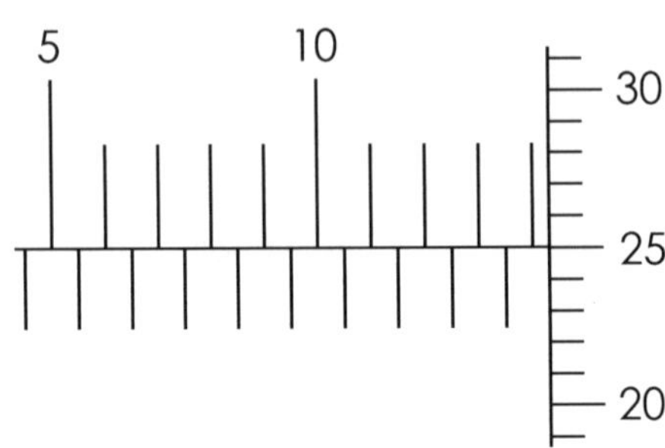

3. Calculate the total **impulse** (change in momentum) from the graph below.

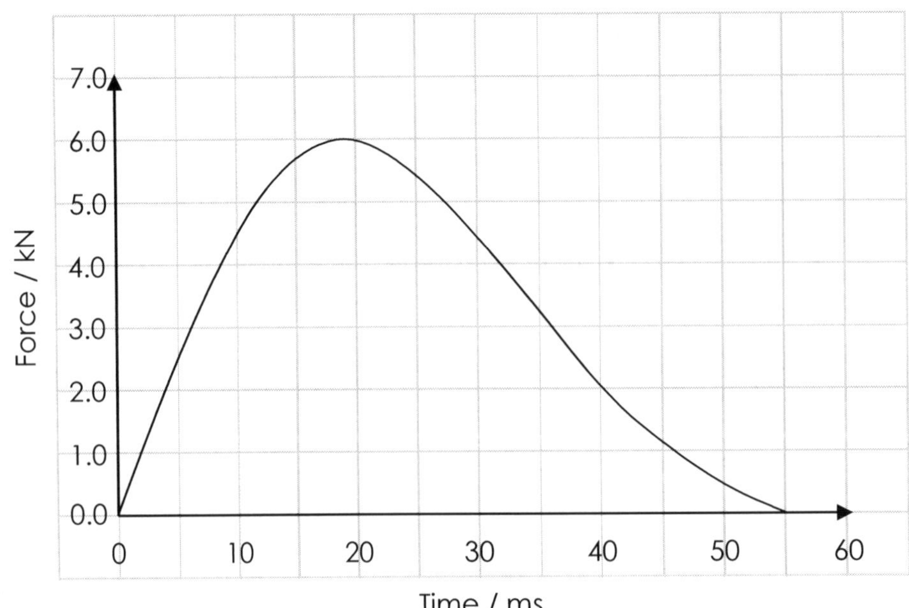

20th January

1 2 3

1. Convert the following volumes into **m³** :

    a. 10.0 cm^3

    b. 1.0 ltr

    c. 3.3 decilitres

    d. 500 ml

2. A projectile is launched at an angle of 60° above the horizontal with a velocity of 50 m s^{-1}. Calculate the **maximum** height reached by the projectile.

3. Two speakers, A and B, emit sound waves at a speed of 330 m s^{-1} and a frequency of 550 Hz. The two sound waves meet at a position that is 1.20 m from speaker A and 1.50 m from speaker B. **State** and **explain** what is heard at that position.

21st January

1 2 3

1. Write down the **value** and **units** for the following constants:

    a. Planck's constant

    b. Boltzmann constant

    c. Molar gas constant

2. Purple light of wavelength 380 nm interferes after passing through slits of separation 0.25 mm. Calculate the **spacing** between two maxima on a screen 2.50 m away.

3. A 45 g golf ball is struck with a club face. The force-time graph is shown for this below.

    Calculate the **speed** of the ball as it leaves the tee.

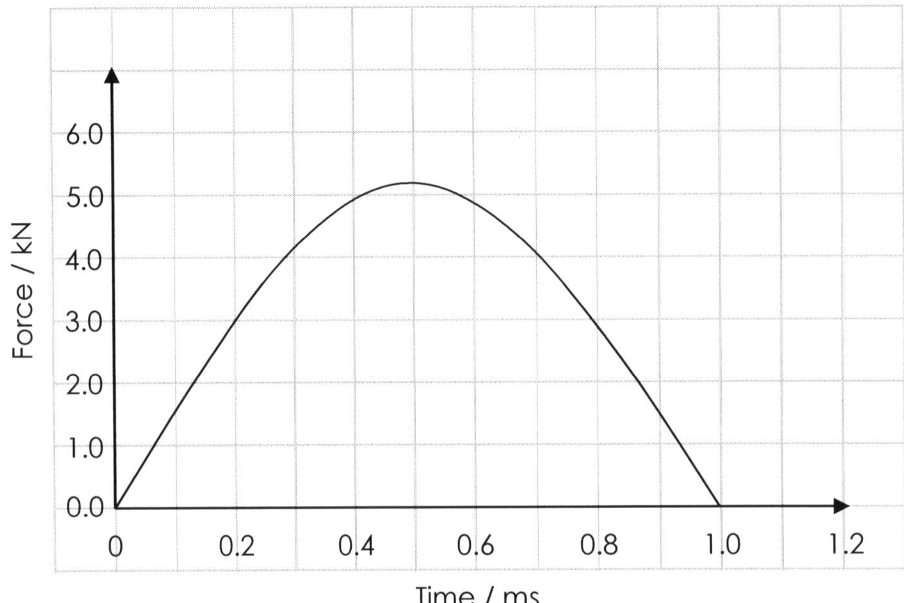

22nd January

1. Sketch a **sinusoidal** curve for the following graphs:

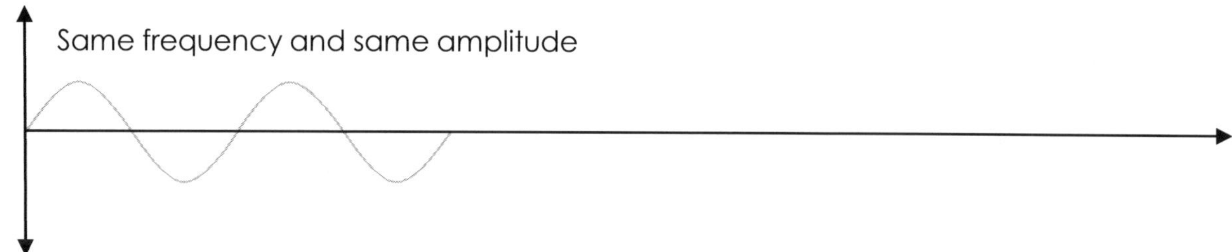

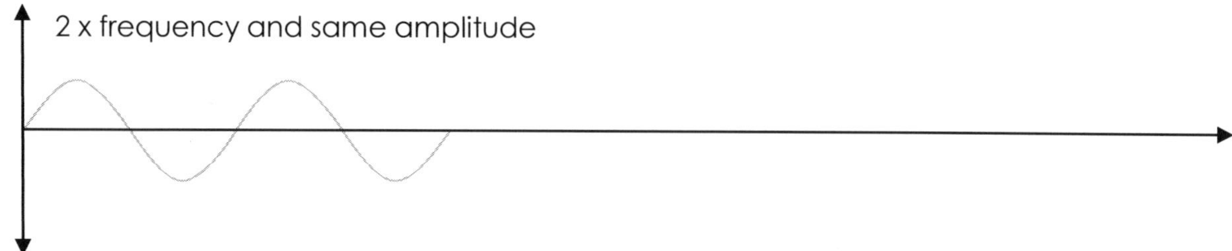

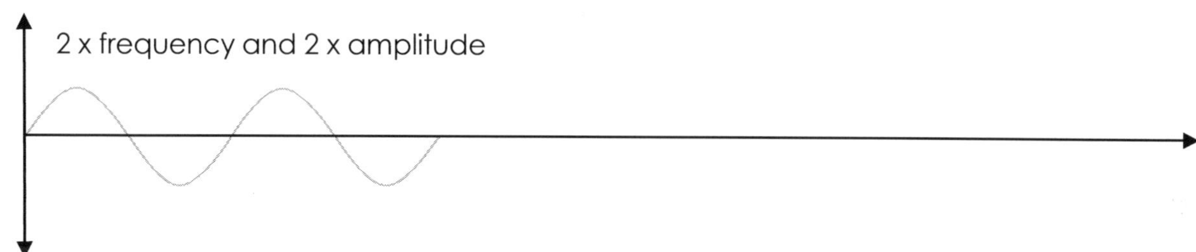

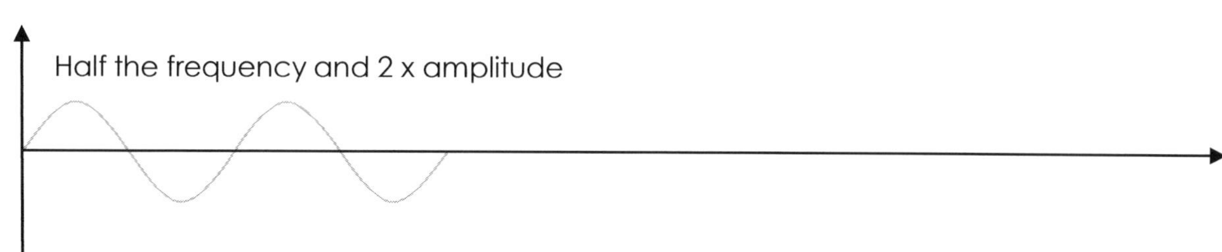

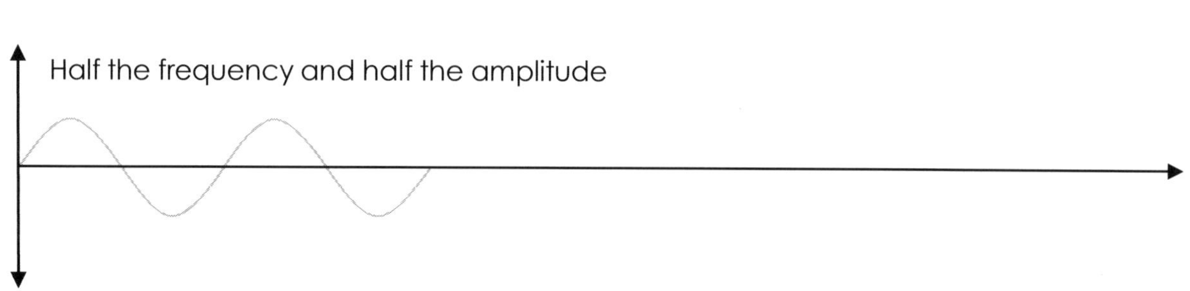

23rd January

1 2 3

1. The half-life of the radioactive isotope lawrencium-262 is 4.0 hours. The number of original nuclei in a sample is 6.4×10^{10}. Calculate the **number** of nuclei left after 1 day.

2. A diffraction grating has 200 lines mm^{-1}. A red laser of wavelength 700 nm is directed onto the grating. Calculate the **maximum** order that can be viewed on a screen.

3. Calculate the total **displacement** of the object in the graph below.

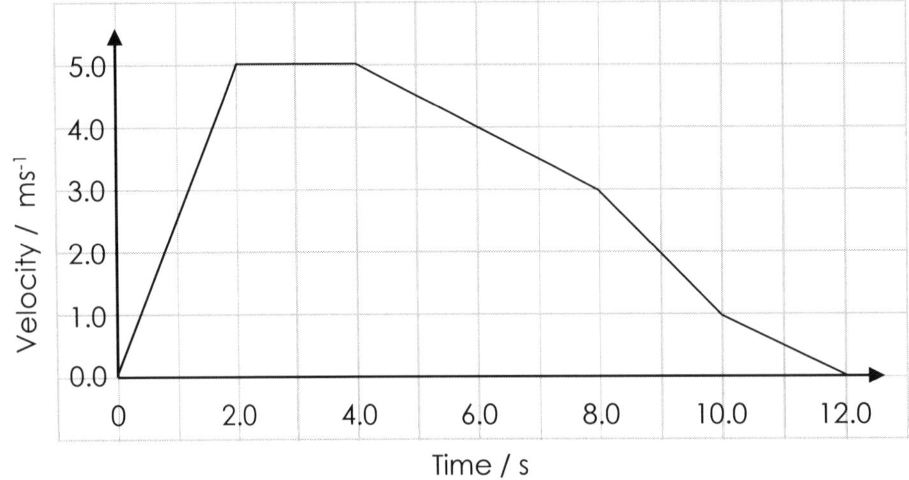

24th January

1 2 3

1. Write down the **value** and **units** for the following constants:

   a. Gravitational constant

   b. Stefan's constant

   c. Atomic mass unit

2. Read the **quantity** measured in the following diagrams of vernier scales.

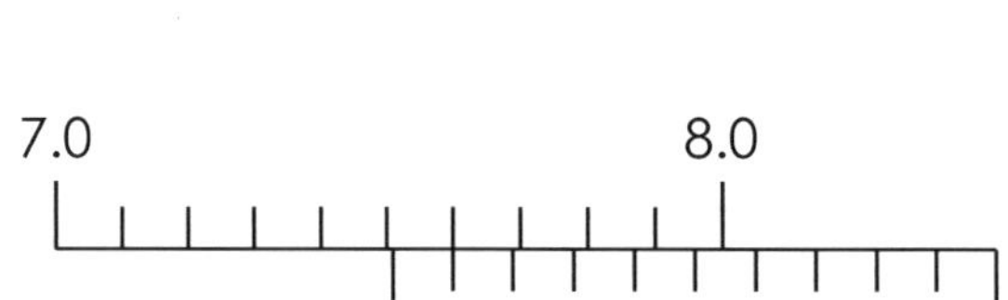

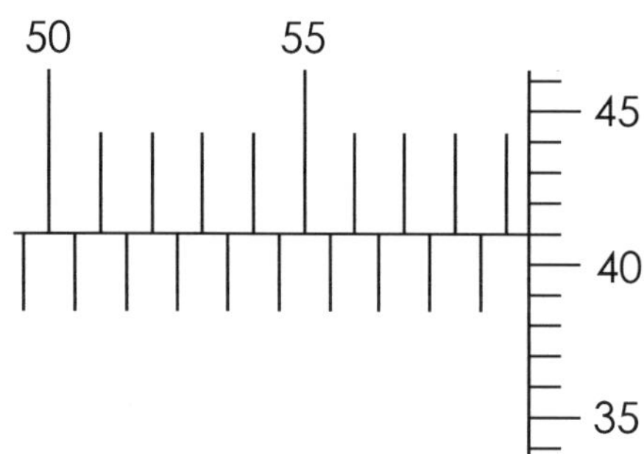

3. Calculate the total **displacement** of the object in the v-t graph below.

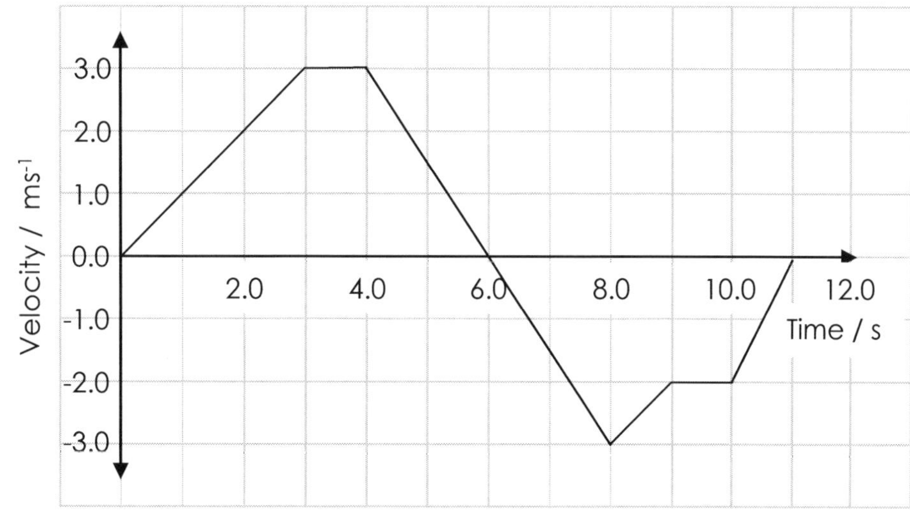

25th January

1 2 3

1. State **three** ways in which all electromagnetic waves are similar.

2. A load of 120 N is applied to a SWG 25 copper wire. Calculate the **tensile stress** in the wire.

3. Calculate the total **displacement** of the object in the v-t graph below.

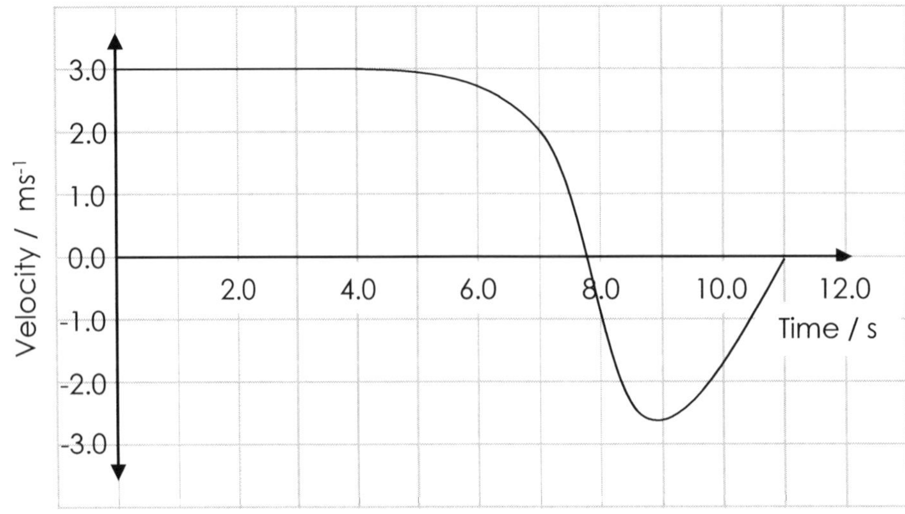

26th January – Part 1

1. Sketch the corresponding **velocity-time** graph to this displacement-time graph.

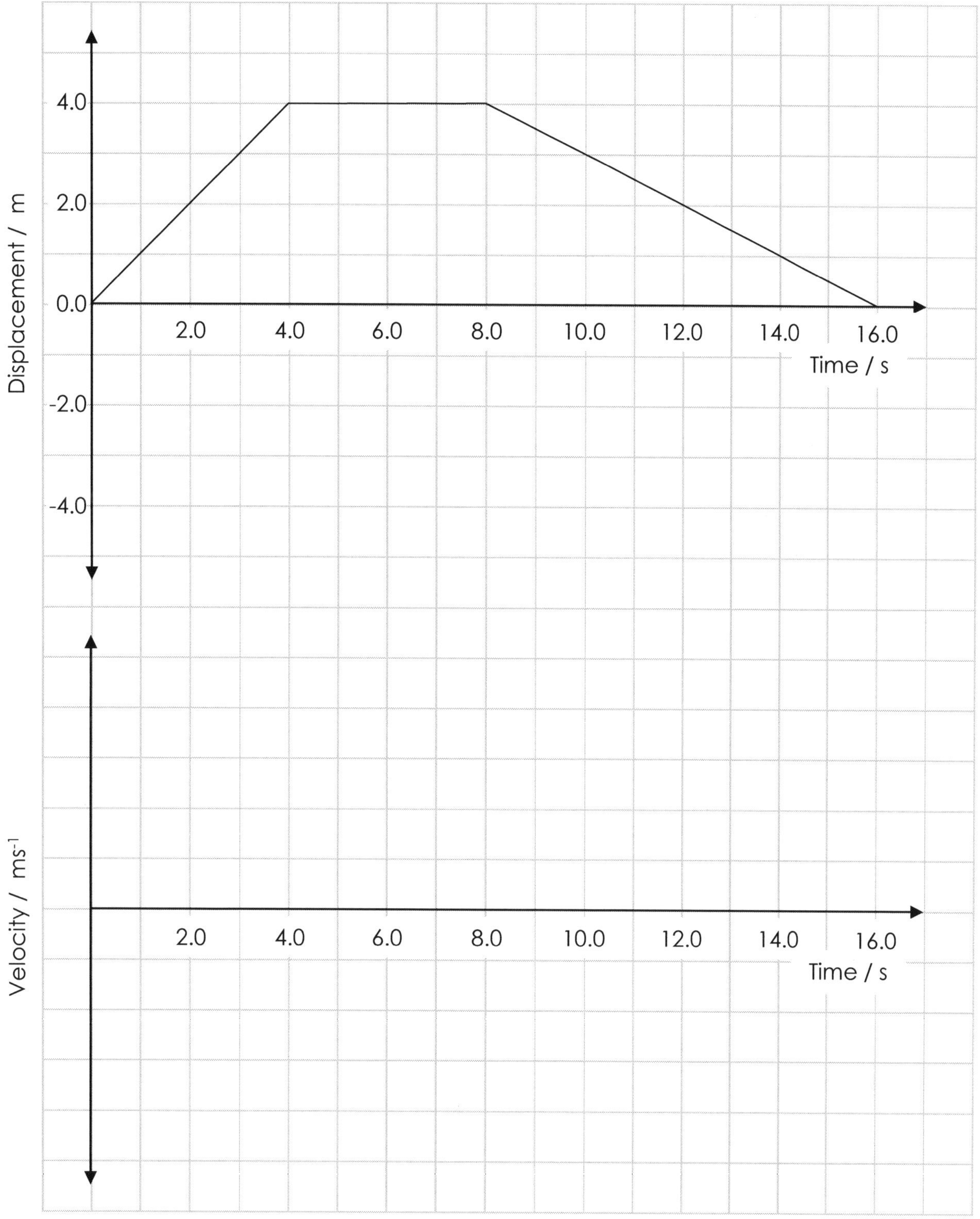

26th January – Part 2

2. Sketch the corresponding **displacement-time** graph to this velocity-time graph.

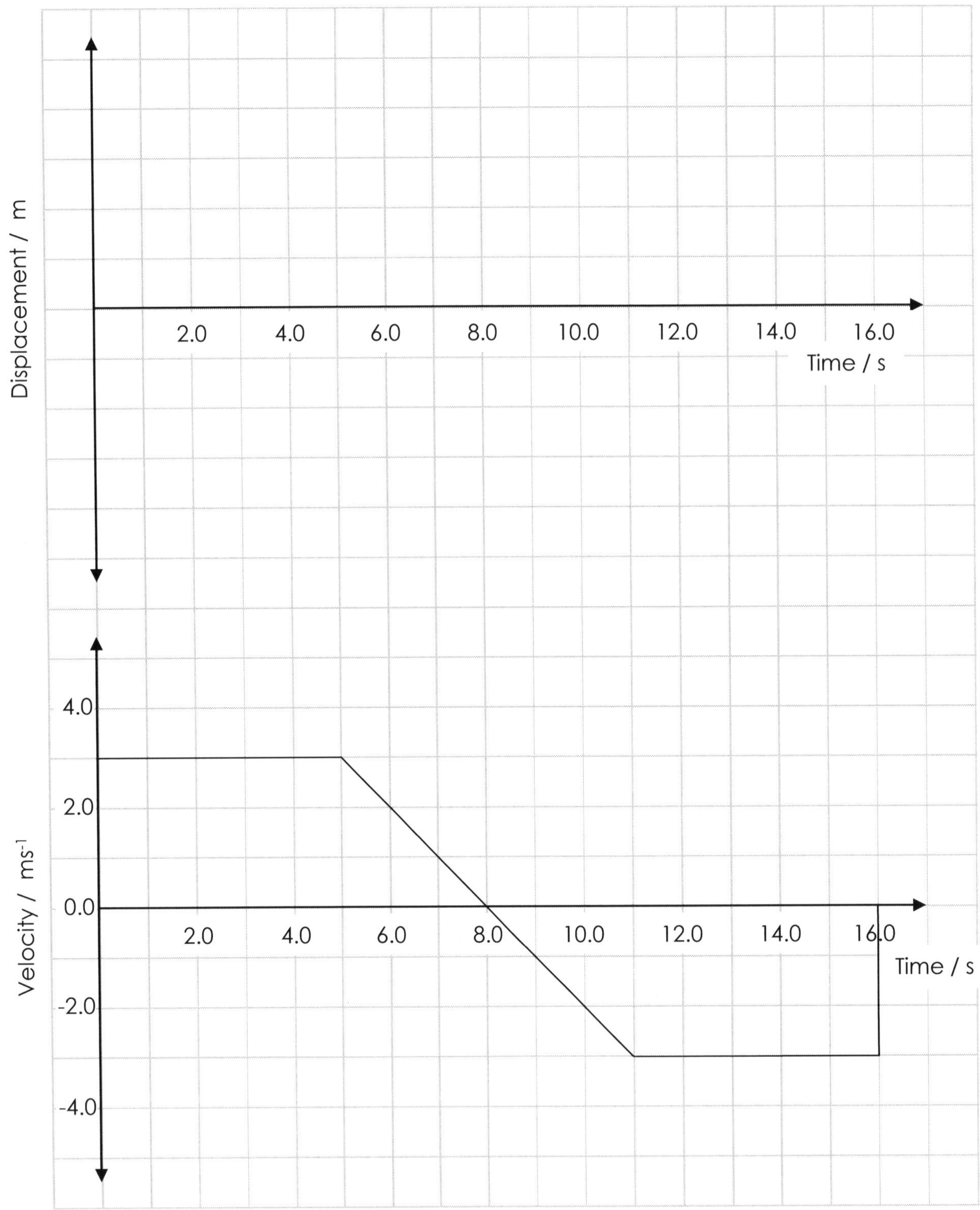

27th January – Part 1

1. Sketch the corresponding **velocity-time** graph to this displacement-time graph.

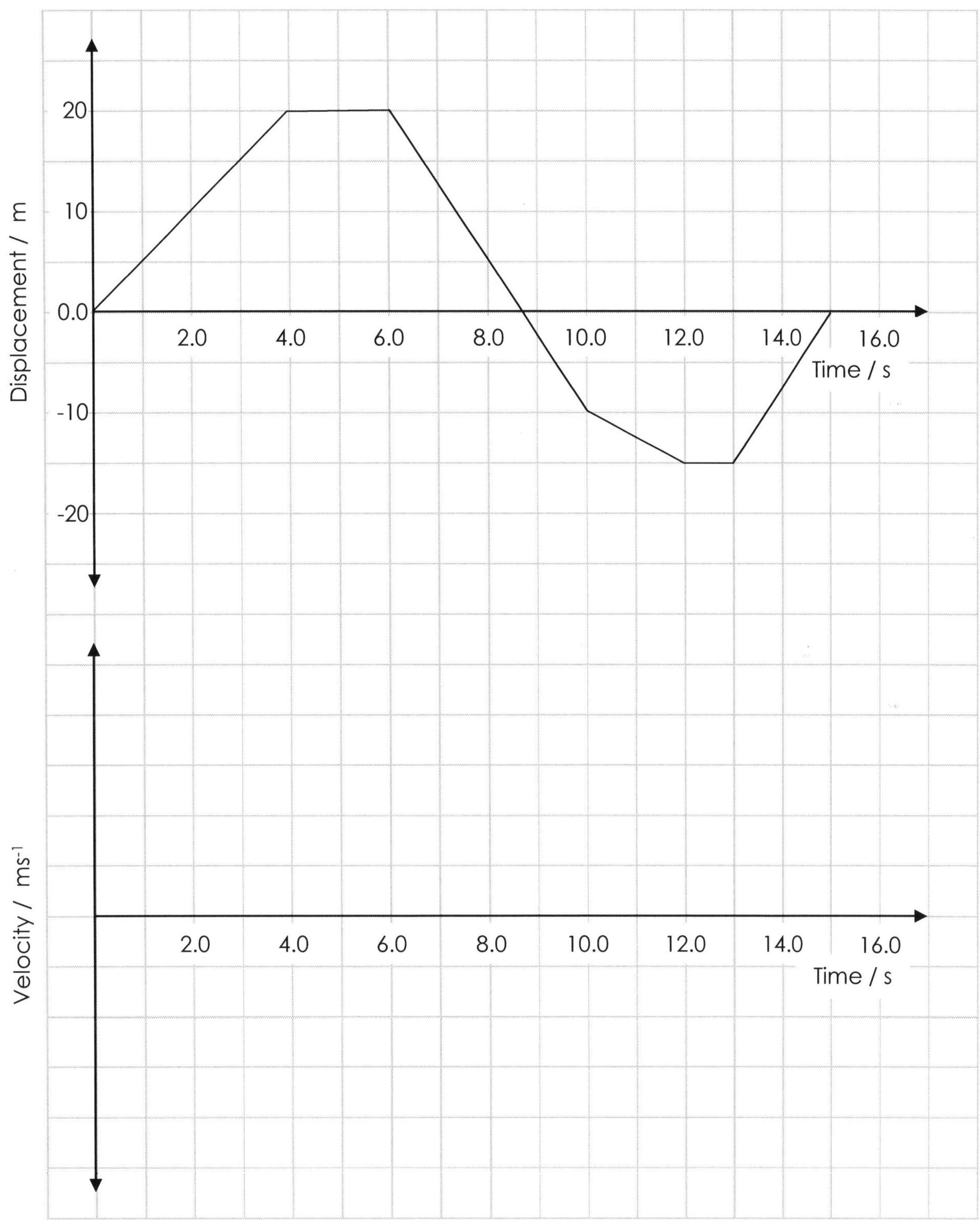

27th January – Part 2

2. Sketch the corresponding **acceleration-time** graph to this velocity-time graph.

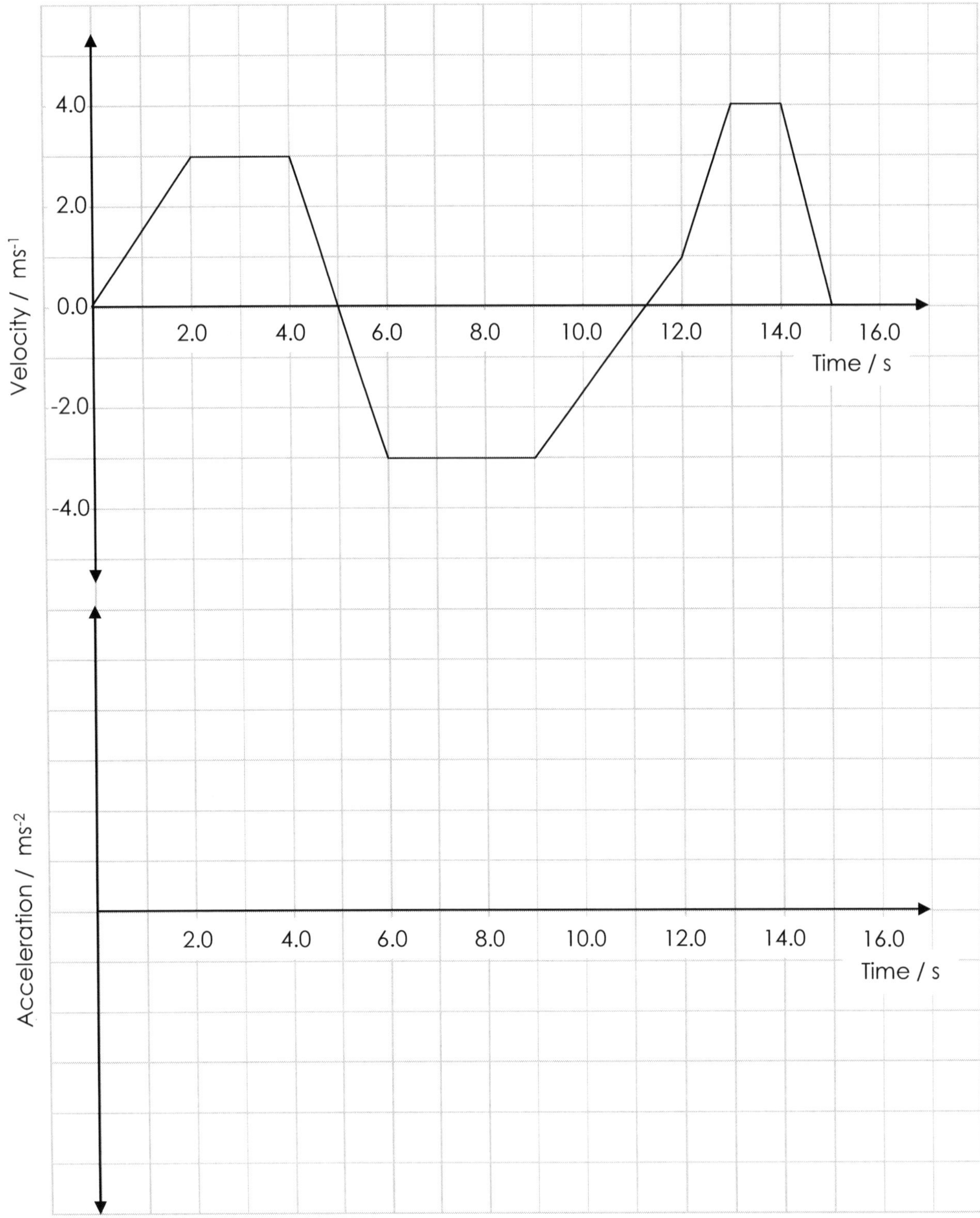

28th January

1 2 3

1. A spring of stiffness 60 N m^{-1} is originally 35 mm long. When extended it stores 40 mJ of elastic potential energy. Calculate the total **length** of the spring.

2. Define:

   a. A **progressive** wave

   b. A **stationary/standing** wave

3. A wire, with a diameter of 0.20 mm and an original length of 30 cm, stretches by 43 mm when a 370 N tensile load is applied.

   Determine the **metal** the wire is made from.

Metal	Young's Modulus / GPa
Gold	77
Silver	83
Bronze	112
Platinum	154

29th January

1 2 3

1. Calculate the **frequency** of:

   a. An X-ray (also called Röntgen radiation) with wavelength 0.021 nm

   b. Infrared radiation of wavelength 1064 nm

   c. Red light

2. State the **masses** (in kg), **charges** (in C) and **penetrating** ability of alpha, beta minus and gamma radiation.

3. The shoe is at **rest** on a slope. Calculate the size of the **friction** acting up the slope if it has a mass of 575 g and θ = 36˚.

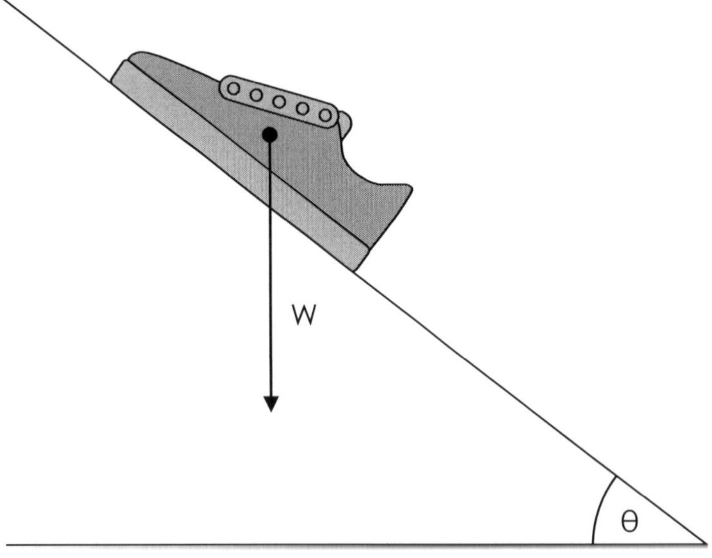

30th January

1 2 3

1. Write down the **value** and **units** for the following constants:

   a. Planck's constant

   b. Boltzmann constant

   c. Molar gas constant

2. A ray of light is travelling through a glass block. The wavelength of the light is 450 nm and the frequency is 5.1×10^{14} Hz.

   Calculate the **refractive index** of the glass.

3. Two gliders on an air track have masses m_1 = 131 g and m_2 = 142 g, they travel towards each other at 1.21 m s^{-1} and 0.95 m s^{-1} respectively. There is a perfectly inelastic collision.

   Calculate their **final velocity** after they collide.

31st January

1 2 3

1. Write down the **units** for:
    a. Momentum
    b. Resistivity
    c. Work function
    d. Impulse

2. A 1500 kg car initially travelling at 50 km h^{-1} exerts a constant braking force of 5.0 kN.

   Calculate the **braking distance** of the car.

3. Have a look back at questions 1 and 2 from 1st January and the three small goals you made.

   Reflect on the progress you have made towards these goals and the small habits you have implemented.

JANUARY REVIEW

You know the score – reflect on your work in January.

A Level Physics Content	Red	Amber	Green
I can sketch **wavefront** diagrams			
I can recall the values of some common **constants**			
I can use **moments** in **equilibrium** situations			
I can **estimate** the **area** under a graph			
I can **relate** the area under a graph to a physical **quantity**			
I can use **data** from one graph to **plot** a further graph			

Any other comments:

FEBRUARY

FEBRUARY

Take a look at what you have achieved so far. It is impressive! This is all down to you.

The way you approach learning in lessons and the independent work you decide to complete outside of school. Your desire to take ownership of your studying will pay-off. Now you're halfway through your first year of A Level Physics, the results will soon become apparent.

1st February

1 2 3

1. Calculate the **length** of the adjacent side of a triangle with an angle of 18° and an opposite side length of 4.3 cm.

2. A 6.0 V battery, with negligible internal resistance, has two bulbs connected in parallel across it. One bulb has a resistance of 3.0 Ω and the other has a resistance of 6.0 Ω at 6.0 V. Calculate the total **charge** transferred in 30 seconds in the circuit.

3. Sketch the **standing/stationary** wave formed on a 0.65 m **string** fixed at both ends, and state the **wavelength** in each case:

   a. First harmonic

   b. Second harmonic

   c. Third harmonic

2nd February

1 2 3

1. A resistor has a resistance of 47 Ω. Calculate the **current** flowing through the resistor if there is a potential difference of 1.2 V across it.

2. Define:

   a. **Kirchhoff's first** law

   b. **Kirchhoff's second** law

3. Sketch the **standing/stationary** wave formed in the 0.80 m **tube** open at one end, and state the **wavelength** in each case:

   a. First harmonic

   b. Second harmonic

   c. Third harmonic

3rd February

1. A 20 000 N draw bridge can be modelled as a uniform beam. Initially it is horizontal, supported at B and able to pivot about A.

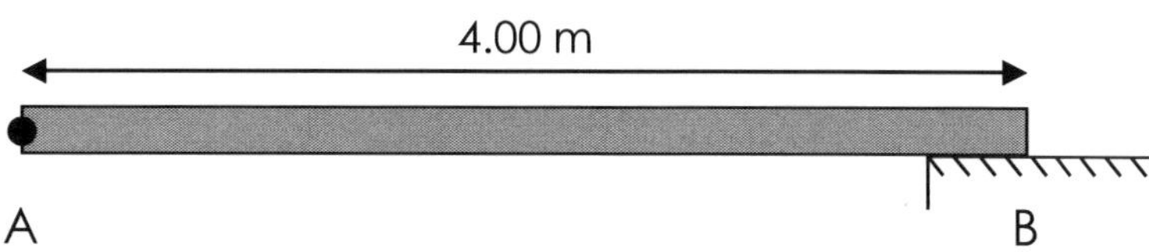

a. Calculate the **clockwise moment** about point A in this position

b. Calculate the **clockwise moment** if the drawbridge is raised to **45.0˚** above the horizontal

The drawbridge is raised from horizontal to vertical at a constant rate of 2.0˚ every second.

c. Plot a graph of **clockwise moment against time** as the drawbridge is raised

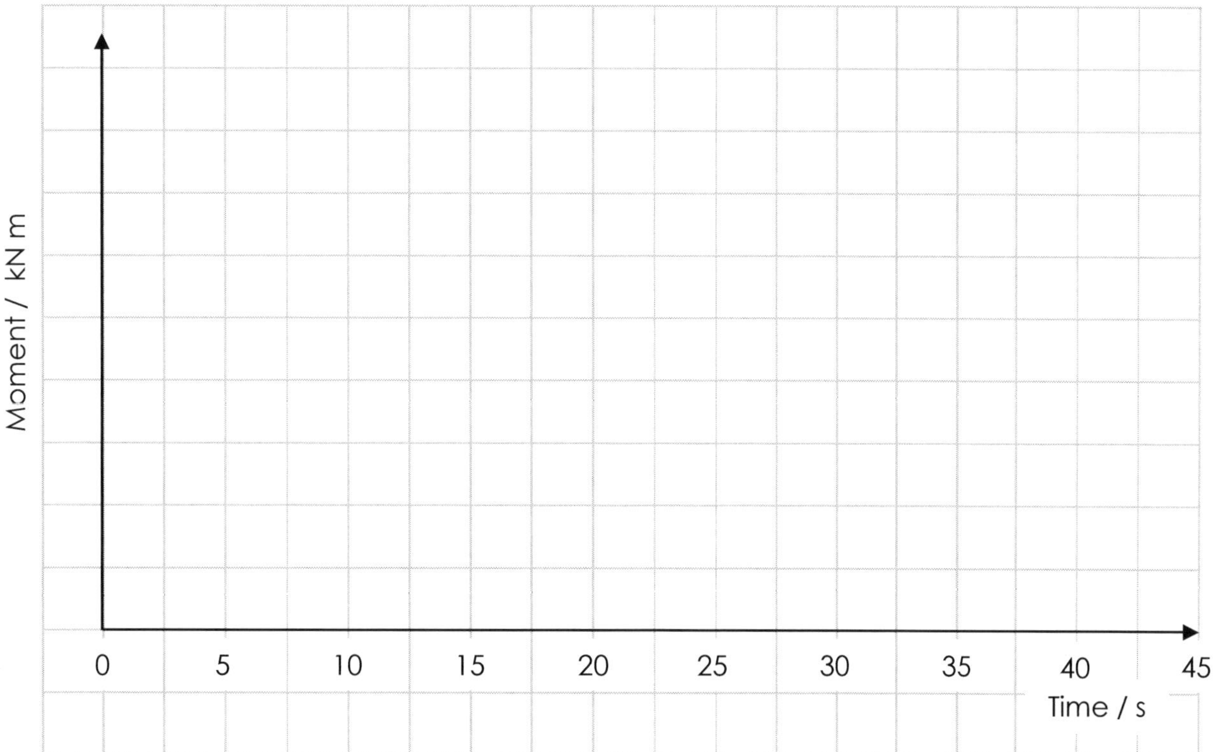

4th February

1 2 3

1. Write down the **value** and **units** for the following constants:

   a. Electron rest mass

   b. Avogadro's number

   c. Wien's constant

2. The energy of a photon is related to its frequency.

   a. Rearrange $E = hf$ to make **h** the **subject**

   b. State:
      i. Planck's **constant**

      ii. The Planck **length**

      iii. The Planck **time**

3. a. Define what a **superconductor** is

   b. Give examples of where they are used

   c. Explain why 'high-temperature' superconductors are very useful.

5th February

1 2

1. The EMF of a battery is 4.5 V. An ammeter in series with a resistor records a current of 1.2 A when the terminal potential difference drops to 4.2 V. Calculate the **internal resistance** of the battery.

2. Two coherent waves P and Q are in phase. They interfere and superpose. Sketch the **resultant wave**.

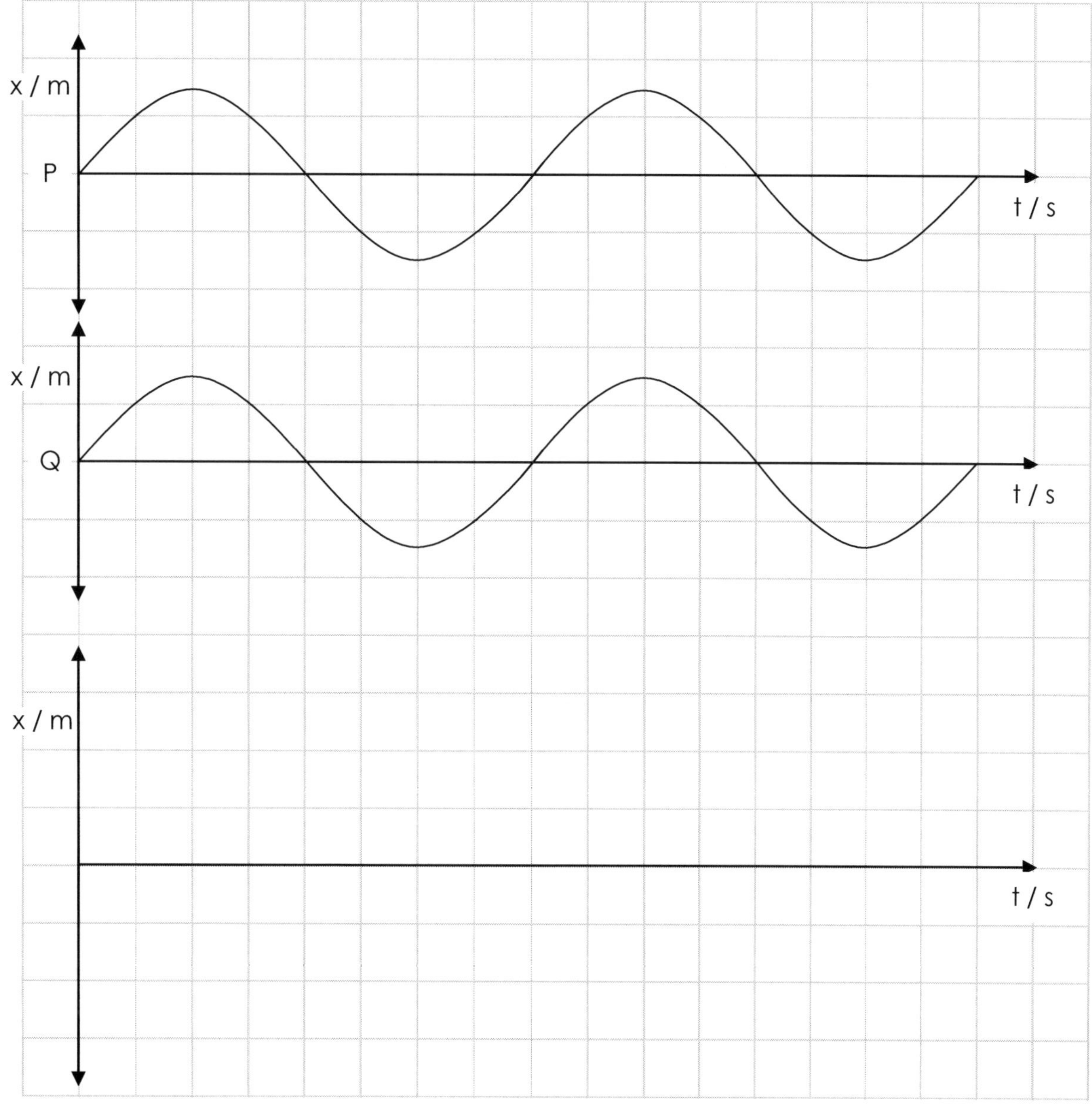

6th February

1 2

1. Quarks are a type of fundamental particle. State how **many** there are, their **names** and their **charges**.

2. Two coherent waves P and Q are out of phase by 180˚. They interfere and superpose. Sketch the **resultant wave**.

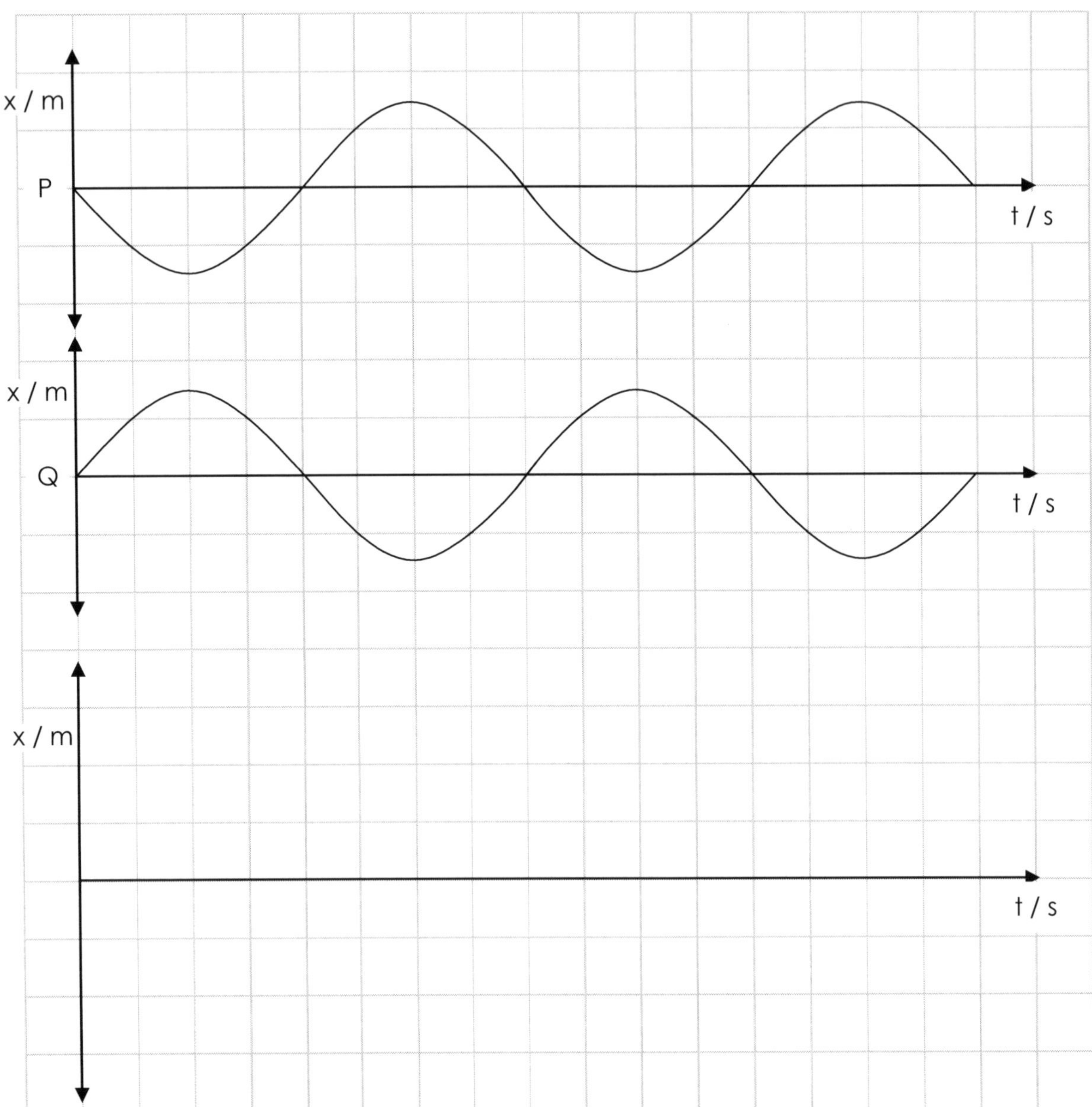

7th February

1 2 3

1. Write the following quantities using an **appropriate** prefix:

   a. 0.000 000 630 m

   b. 1 320 000 000 W

   c. 40 200 000 000 000 J

   d. 0.0420 s

2. Define:

   a. An **elastic** collision

   b. A **perfectly inelastic** collision

3. Calculate the **internal resistance** of the cell in the circuit below.

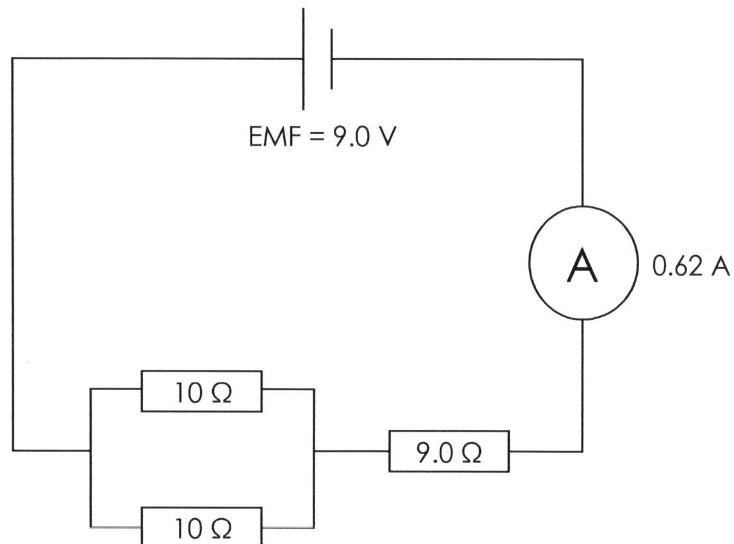

8th February

1 2

1. Write the following in **standard form**:

   a. 0.000 010 2 km

   b. 84 000 pm

   c. 0.203 GeV

   d. 0.797 Mpc

2. Two coherent waves P and Q are out of phase by π/2 radians. They interfere and superpose. Sketch the **resultant wave**.

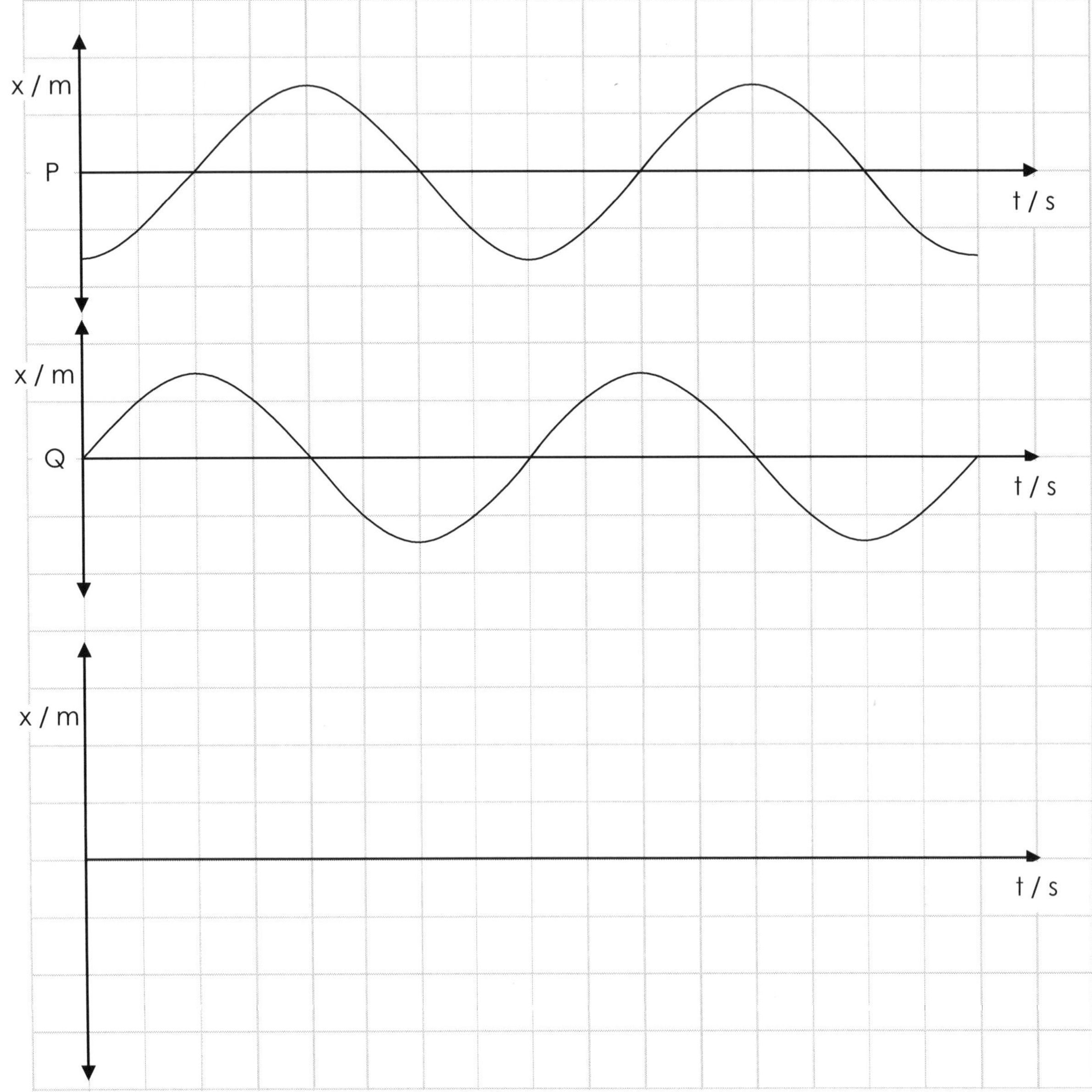

Make sure you order your copy of the next book ready for 1st March!

Get prepared for your exams

9th February

1 2 3

1. Define what the term '**rest energy**' means for a particle.

2. List the **apparatus** and **safety precautions** required to measure the wavelength of light using a diffraction grating.

3. A transformer has potential differences of 230 V and 12 V across the primary and secondary coils respectively. It has a current of 10 A in the primary coil and 120 A in the secondary coil.

   Calculate the **efficiency** of the transformer.

10th February

1 2

1. Resolve this 8.0 N force into its **horizontal** and **vertical** components.

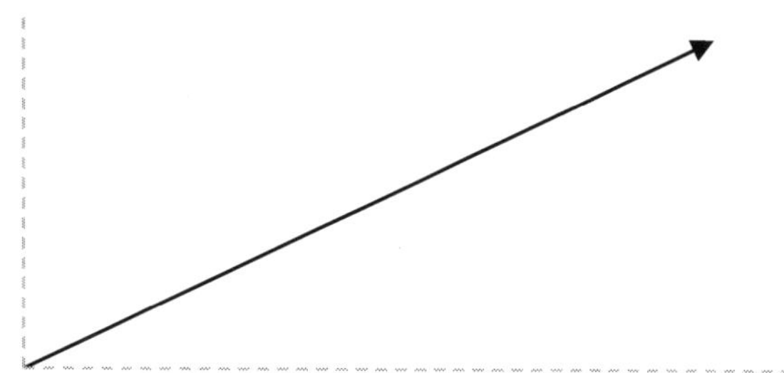

2. Two waves P and Q are shown below. They interfere and superpose. Sketch the **resultant wave**.

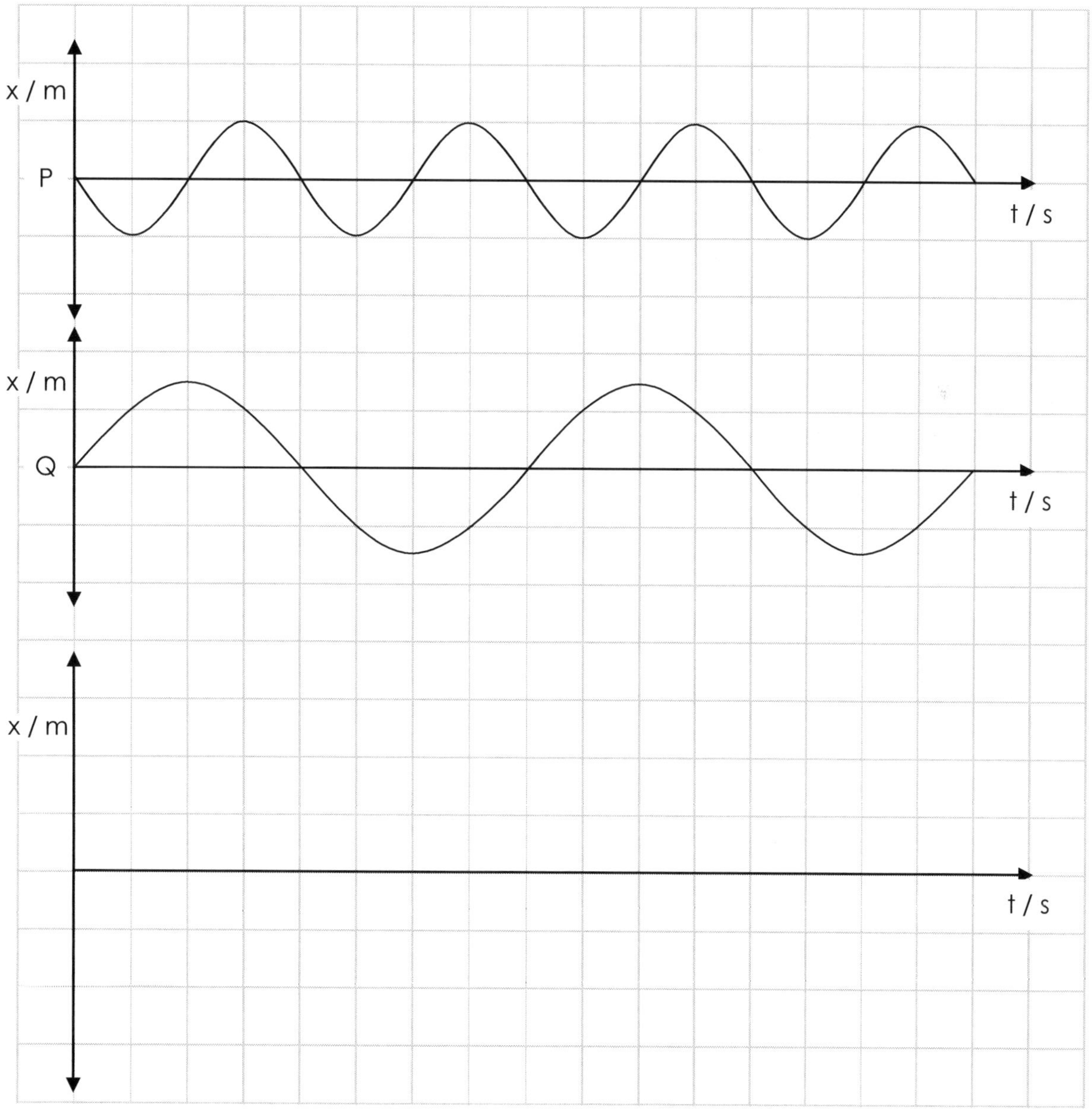

x / m
P
t / s

x / m
Q
t / s

x / m
t / s

11th February

1 2 3

1. Resolve this 29 m s^{-1} velocity into its **northerly** and **easterly** components.

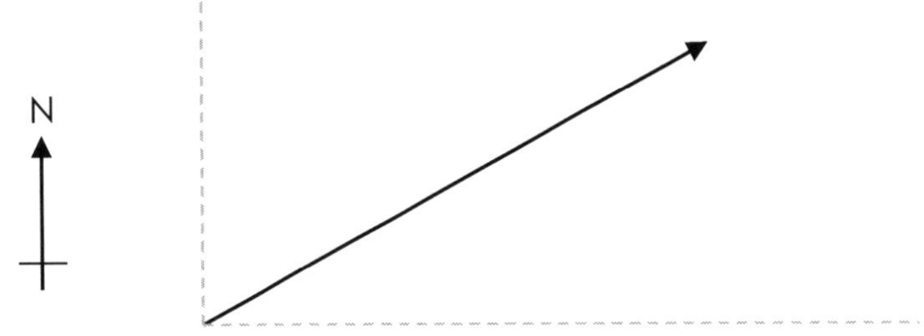

2. Read the **quantity** measured in the following diagrams of vernier scales.

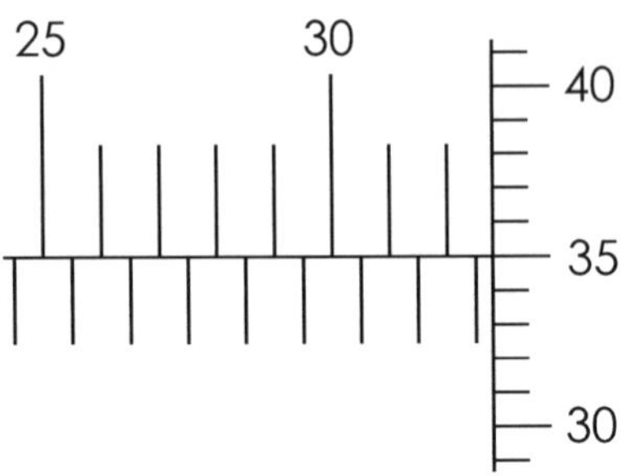

3. Complete the table for the **circuit below** (the battery has negligible internal resistance):

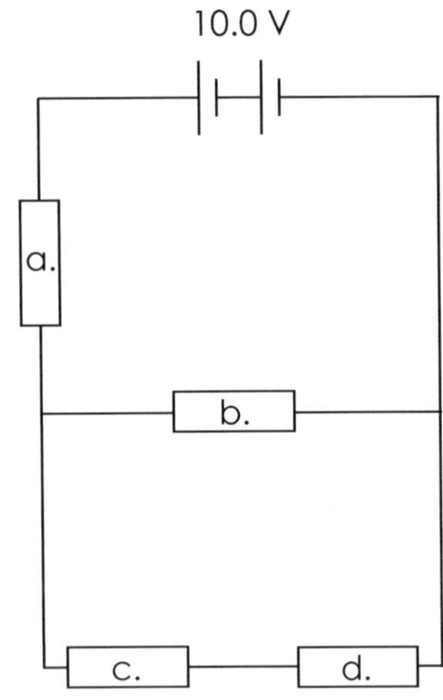

Resistor	R / Ω	V / V	I / A
a.	5.0		
b.		4.1	0.18
c.			
d.		2.2	

12th February

1 2 3

1. Underline the **vector** quantities:

Resistivity	Acceleration	Upthrust
Momentum	Young's modulus	Strain
Current	Electronvolt	Planck's constant

2. Microwaves of wavelength 1.5 mm pass through a double slit. An interference patten is detected 2.0 m away with the distance between points of constructive interference equal to 6.0 cm. Calculate the **slit separation**.

3. Complete the table for the **circuit below** (the battery has negligible internal resistance):

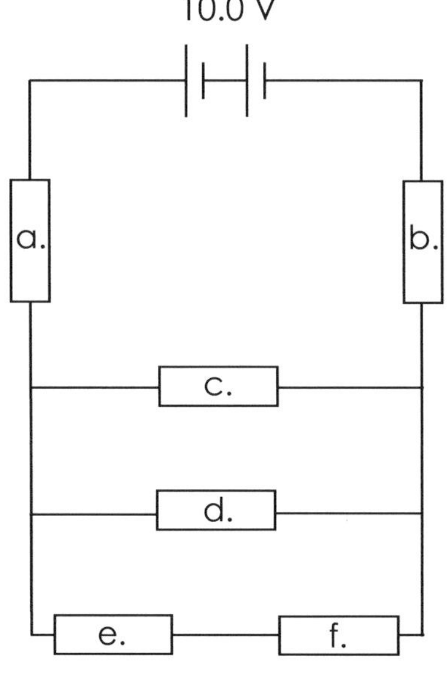

Resistor	R / Ω	V / V	I / A
a.	5.0		
b.		2.2	
c.	41		
d.	41	4.1	
e.		1.0	
f.			

13th February

1. Underline the **scalar** quantities:

Velocity	Time period	Drag
Impulse	Potential difference	Pressure
Displacement	Density	Work done

2. A DC current of 200 mA flows through a lamp that is switched on for 2.0 minutes. Calculate how many **electrons** flow past a point in the circuit.

3. Calculate the **percentage uncertainty** in the **y-intercept**.

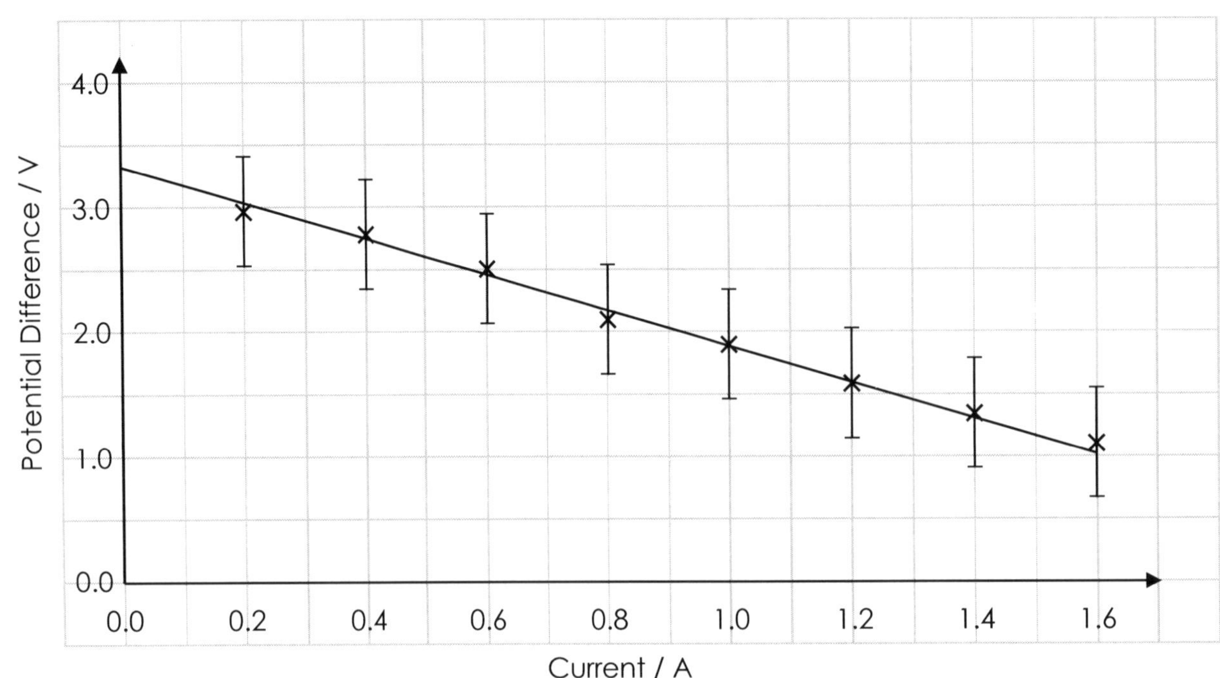

14th February

1 2 3

1. A bungee rope of spring constant 200 N m^{-1} is extended by a distance of 35 m. Calculate the **force** (in units of kN) that is applied to the bungee.

2. Blue laser light is investigated with a double slit arrangement. Calculate the **percentage uncertainty** in the wavelength.

Quantity	Percentage Uncertainty
Slit separation	4.2 %
Fringe spacing	3.1 %
Distance to screen	0.1 %

3. Complete the table for the **circuit below** (each cell has negligible internal resistance and an EMF of 1.5 V):

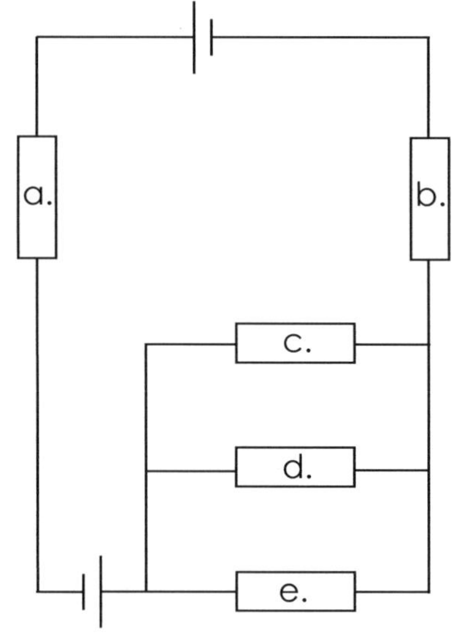

Resistor	R / Ω	V / V	I / A
a.	22		
b.	47		
c.	18		
d.	30		
e.	10		

15th February

1 2 3

1. Calculate the **surface area** of a sphere with a radius of:

   a. 1.0 mm

   b. 1.0 cm

   c. 1.0 m

2. Light is radiated equally in all directions from a 60 W ceiling lamp.

   Calculate the **intensity** 2.4 m away from the bulb.

3. A sensor is fitted to a water bottle rocket that is launched from a school field.

   Calculate the **maximum acceleration** from the velocity-time graph below.

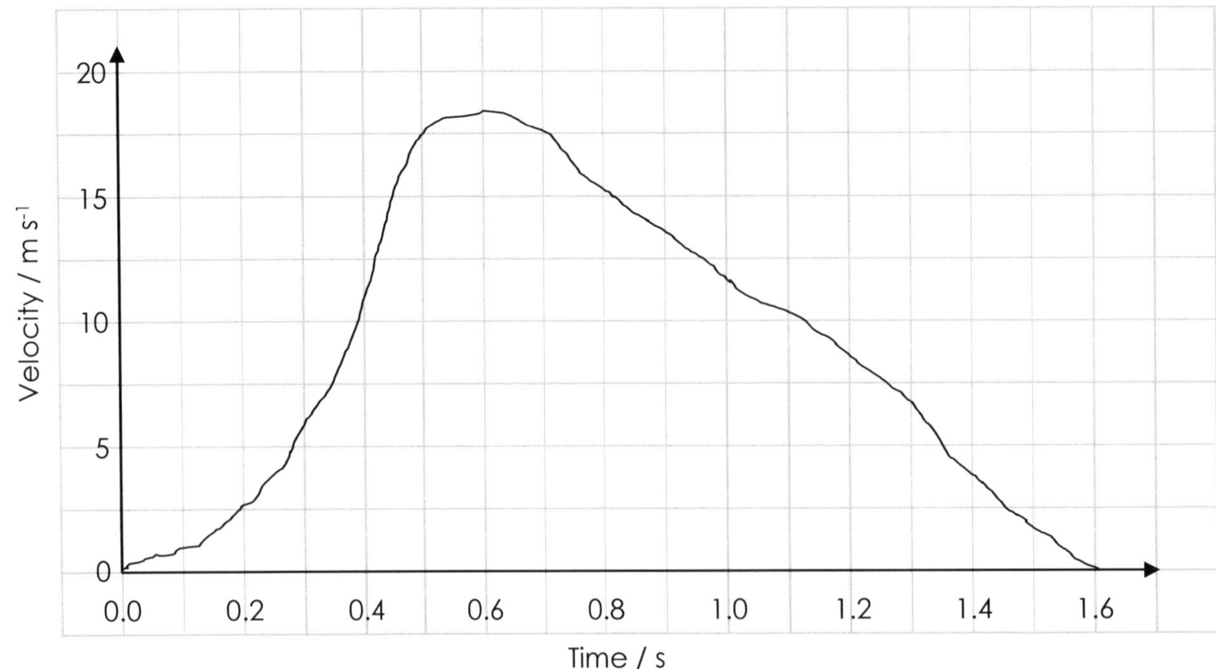

16th February

1 2 3

1. Calculate the **energy** of a red photon with wavelength 630 nm.

2. A 9.0 V battery, when connected across two 125 Ω resistors in series, causes a current of 34 mA.

   Calculate the **internal resistance** of the battery

3. A ray of light passes through a semi-circular block and refracts, as shown by the dashed line -------- below.

   Calculate the **refractive index** of the material and complete the **second ray** showing its path as it exits the block.

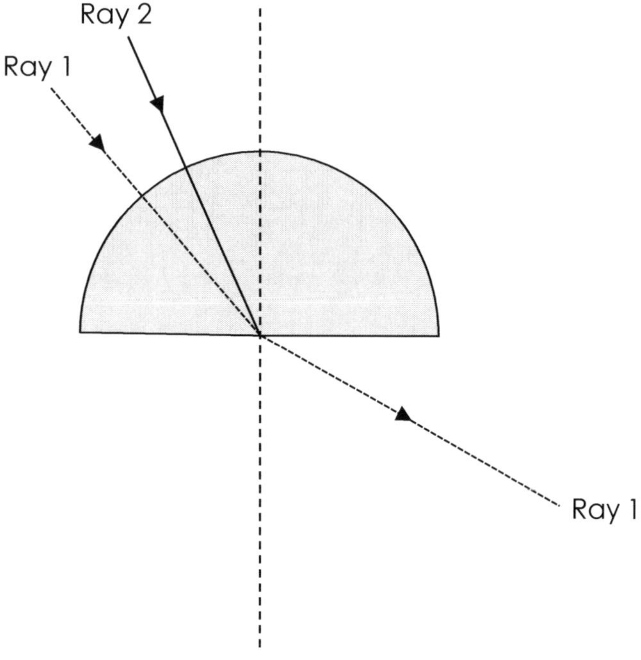

17th February

1 2 3

1. An LED has a current of 0.050 A flowing through it and a potential difference of 1.2 V across it.

   Calculate how much energy the LED transfers in a time of 2.0 minutes.

2. A stone is dropped down a well to estimate its depth. It falls for 3.1 seconds.

   Calculate the **depth** of the well, listing any **assumptions** made.

3. A potential divider circuit is constructed of a 9.0 V battery, 10 000 Ω fixed resistor and a thermistor.

   Calculate the **range** of output potential differences across the fixed resistor between 10 °C and 50 °C.

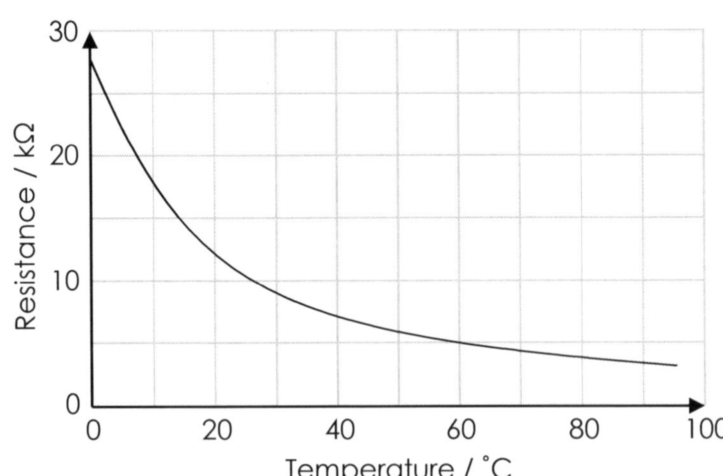

18th February

1. Add a second **sinusoidal** curve for the following displacement-time graphs for a wave:

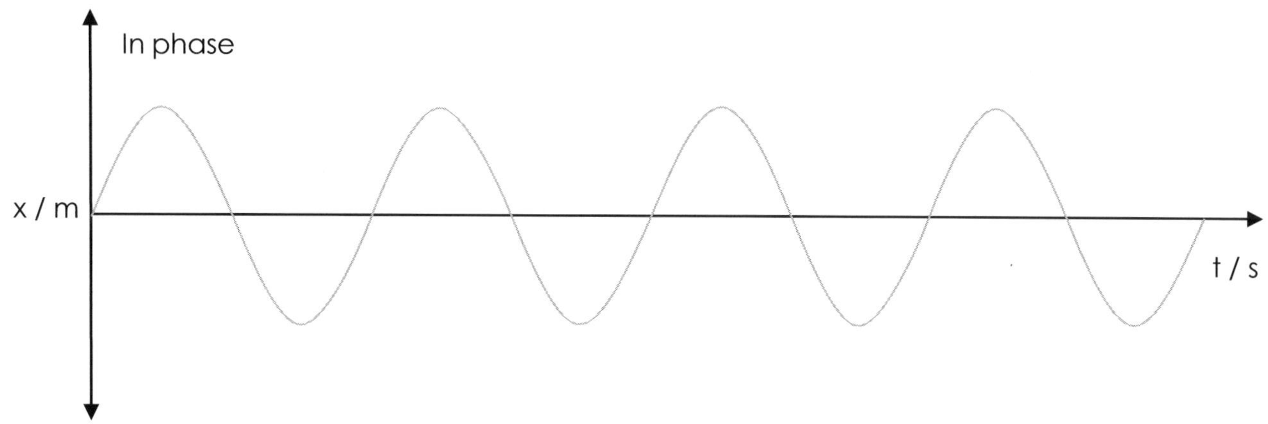

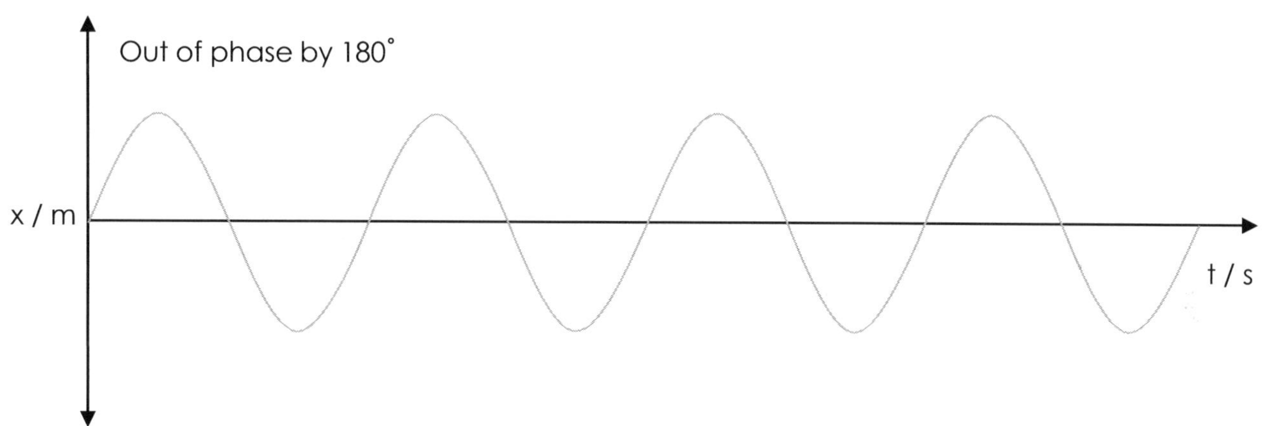

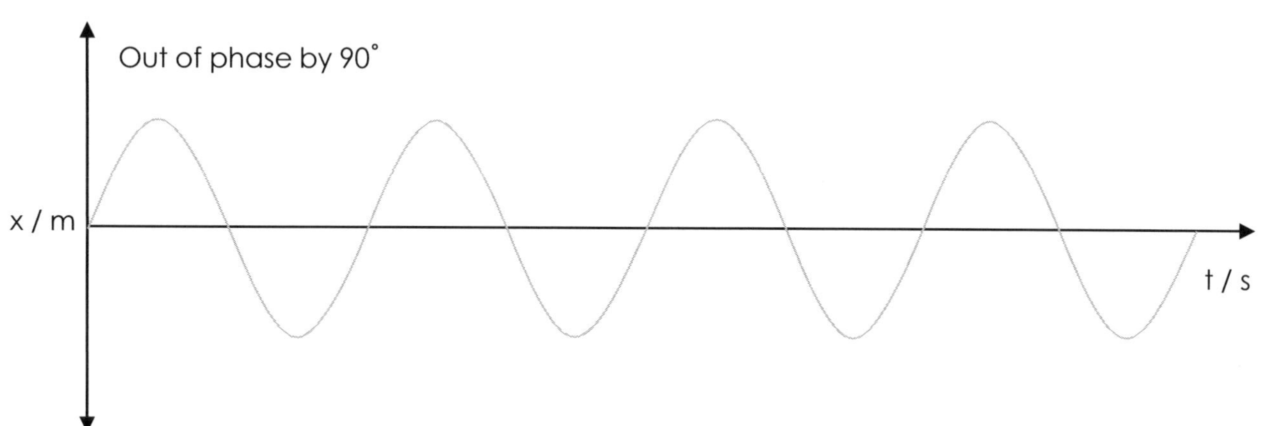

19th February

1 2 3

1. A resistor has 25 C of charge flow through it and a potential difference of 9.0 V across it.

   Calculate the **energy** transferred by the resistor.

2. A Nerf gun is fired vertically into the air from ground level. The 1.02 g dart is in the air for 2.9 seconds.

   Calculate the maximum **gravitational potential energy** gained by the dart.

3. Determine the **amplitude** (in V) and **frequency** of the signal on this oscilloscope trace.

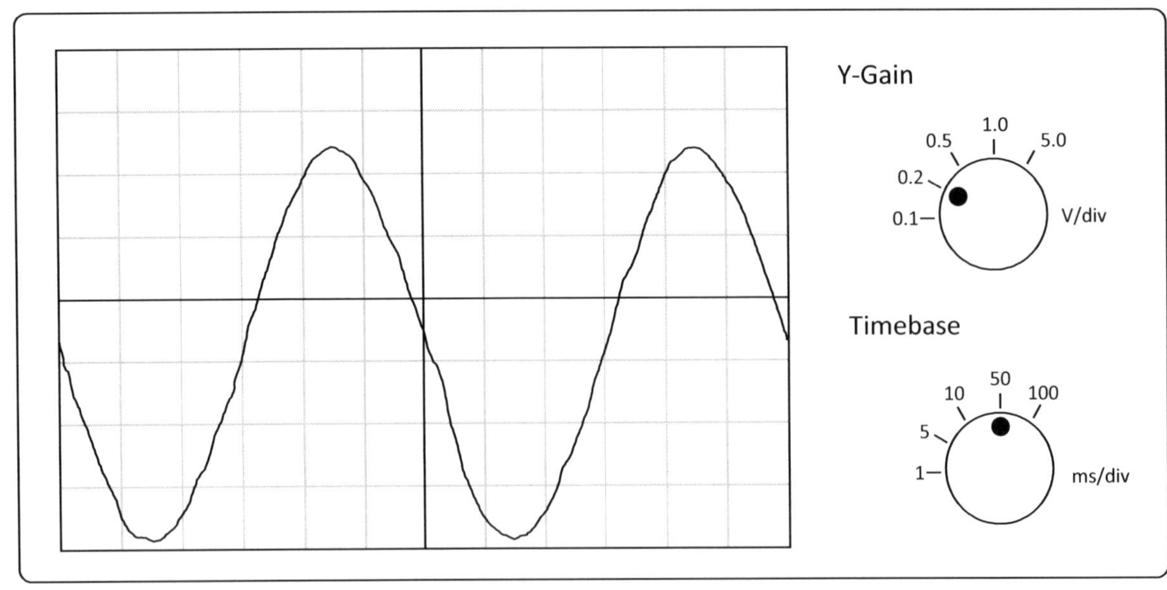

20th February

1 2 3

1. Determine the **result** that should be recorded for m and calculate the **percentage uncertainty** in the data:

m / g	28.2	28.0	26.9	27.3	28.4

2. A bullet is fired horizontally from an SA80 rifle 1.65 m above ground level at 930 m s^{-1}.

   If air resistance is ignored, calculate how **far** the bullet travels before it hits the ground.

3. An electron is accelerated through a potential difference of 3.00 kV in a cathode-ray tube.

   a. Calculate the **kinetic energy** gained by the electron in **eV**

   b. Calculate the **kinetic energy** gained by the electron in **J**

   c. Calculate the **speed** of the electron

21st February

1 2 3

1. Calculate the approximate **energy** of a photon of:

   a. Red light

   b. Green light

   c. Blue light

2. A step index optical fibre is made from two types of glass. Calculate the **critical angle** between the core and the outer layer.

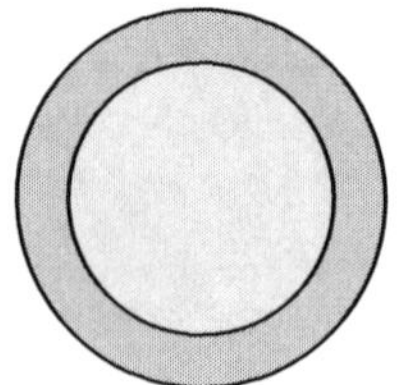
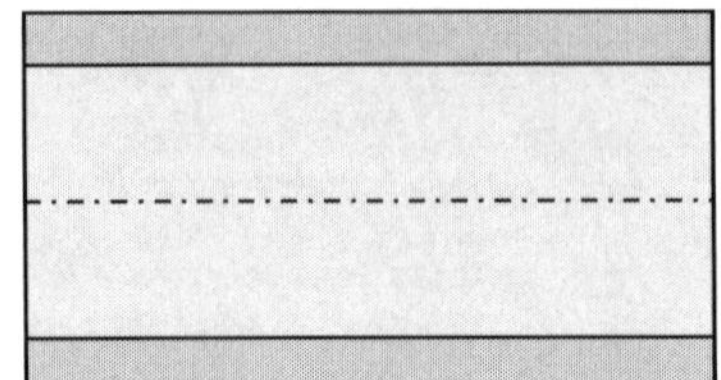

Glass	n
Core	1.45
Outer	1.37

3. A projectile is launched at 10 ms^{-1} from various angles between 0˚ and 90˚. Plot a graph of **launch angle vs. horizontal range** (ignoring air resistance).

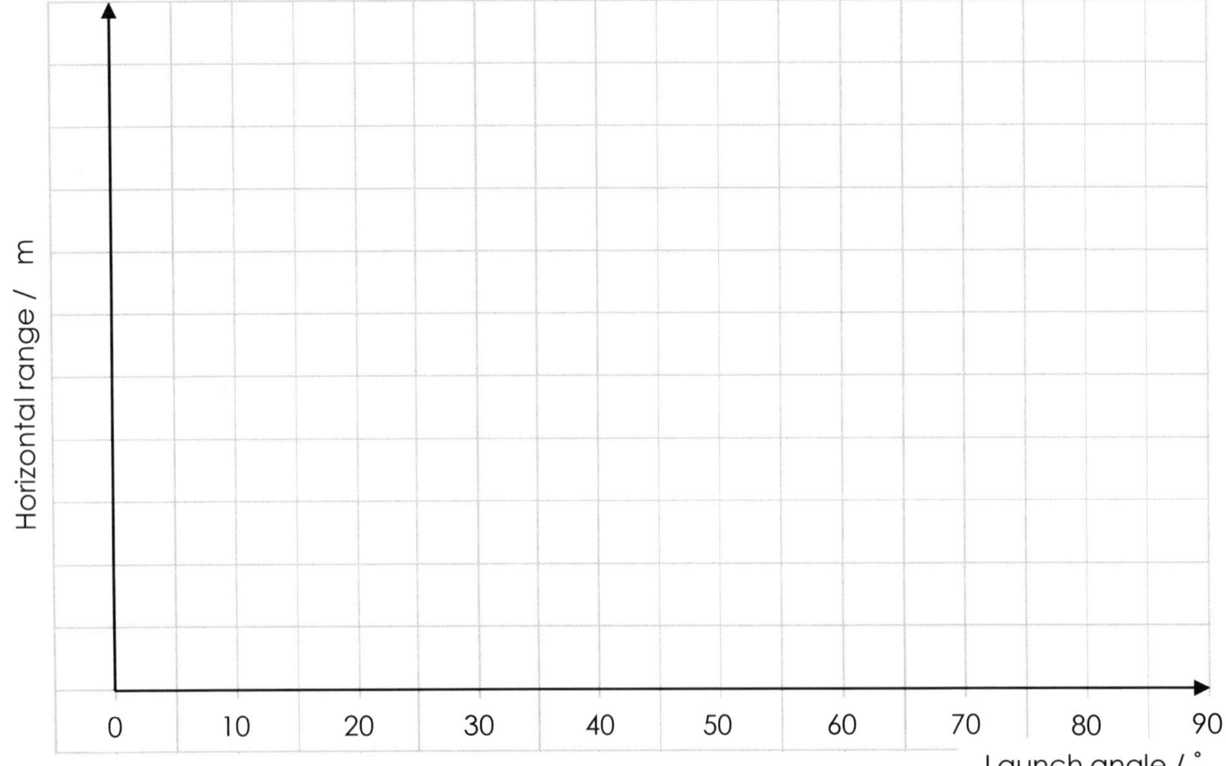

22nd February

1 2

1. A car of mass 1200 kg crashes and decelerates from a velocity of 12 m s^{-1} to rest in a time of 200 ms. Calculate the **average force** experienced by the car in the crash.

2. **Complete** the following table:

	Quantity	Unit	SI Base Units
a.	Mass		
b.	Displacement		
c.	Time		
d.	Velocity		
e.	Acceleration		
f.	Momentum		
g.	Impulse		
h.	Force		
i.	Energy		
j.	Current		
k.	Charge	C	A s
l.	Potential difference		
m.	Resistance		
n.	Temperature		
o.	Specific heat capacity		

23rd February

1. A 'trap door' method is used to determine a value for the acceleration due to gravity. A steel ball bearing of diameter 12 mm is released from an electromagnet. This release starts a digital timer which stops when the ball falls through a 'trap door', breaking a circuit.

   a. Complete the **table**

h / m	t / s	t^2 / s^2
0.200	0.212	
0.300	0.256	
0.400	0.290	
0.500	0.326	
0.600	0.482	
0.700	0.381	

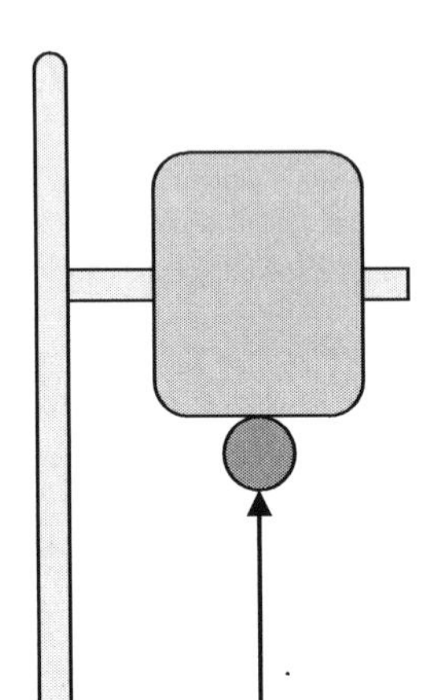

   b. **Plot** the data on the page opposite

   c. Use your graph to **calculate** a value for 'g'

   d. Discuss any **systematic** errors that may occur due to this method

23rd February

24th February

1 2 3

1. Estimate:

    a. The **speed** of a cyclist

    b. The **mass** of a white Ford Transit van

    c. The **weight** of a Lewis Matheson

2. Calculate the **de Broglie wavelength** of an electron travelling at 9.0% of the speed of light.

3. Draw a sinusoidal wave on a **displacement-time** graph with a frequency of 40 Hz and amplitude 5.0 mm. Label the time period and amplitude on your diagram.

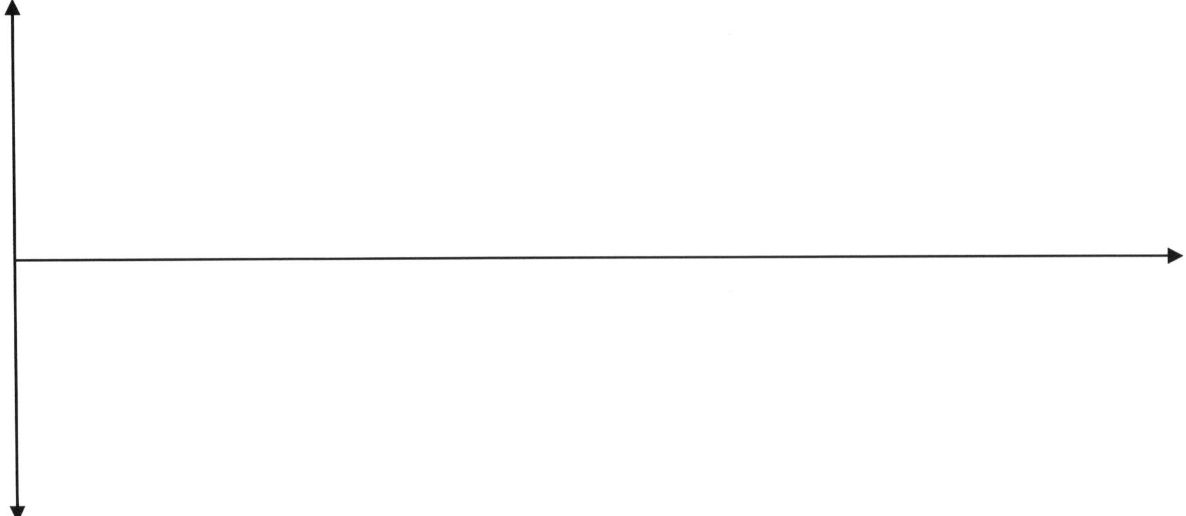

25th February

1 2 3

1. A lamp has a potential difference of 6.0 V across it. It transfers 12 kJ of energy in a time of 15 minutes. Calculate the **current** flowing through the lamp.

2. A stationary fundamental sound wave is set up in a 2.40 m long tube that is closed at both ends.

   Calculate the **wavelength** of the wave and hence its **frequency**.

3. A seagull flies horizontally at 15 m s^{-1} as it ejects guano with a vertical velocity of 5.0 m s^{-1} downwards.

   Calculate the **velocity** (size and direction) of the bird poo as it hits a sunbather lying on a beach 30 m below.

26th February – Part 1

1. Trace the following **curves**.

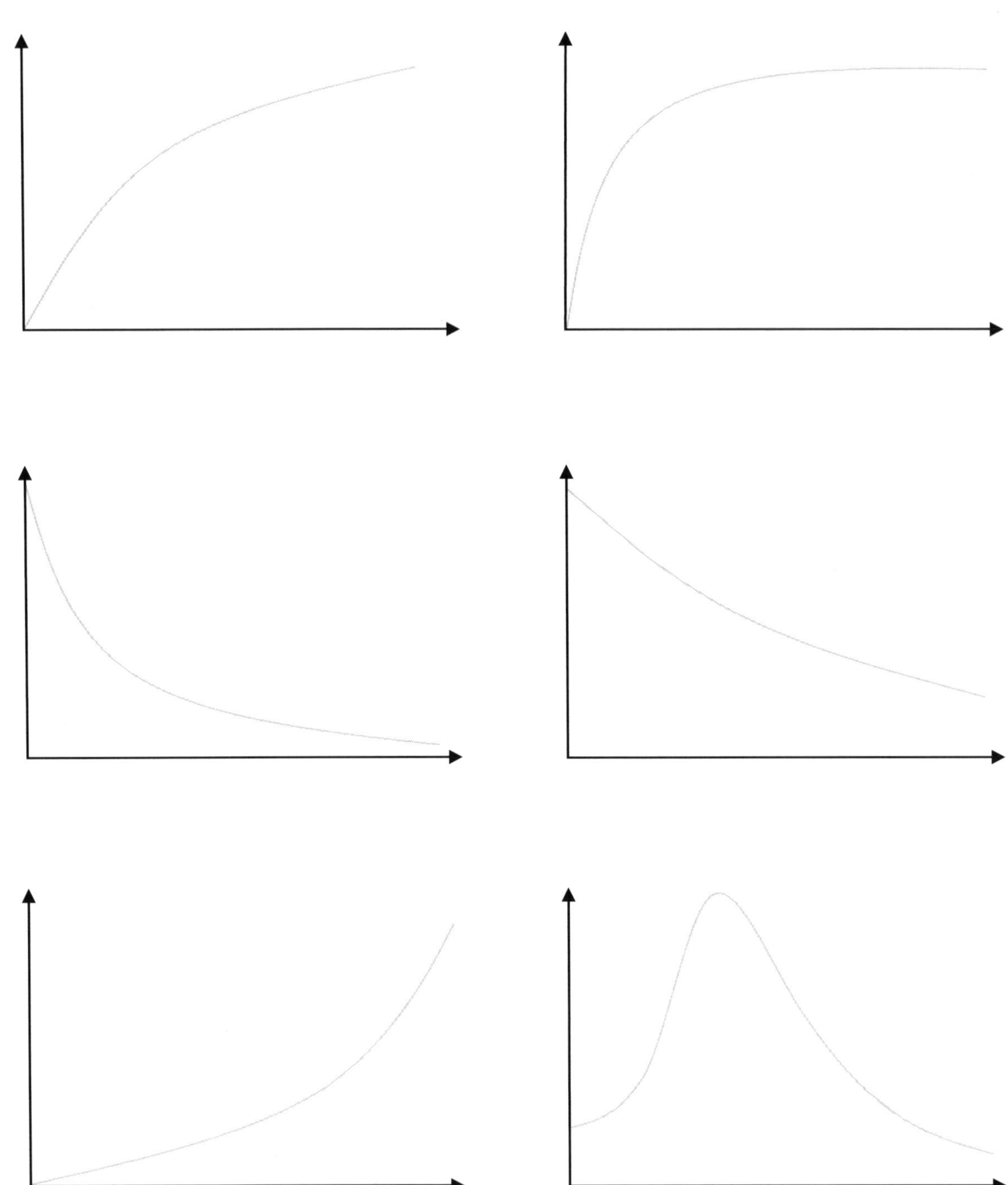

26th February – Part 2

2. Trace the following **curves**.

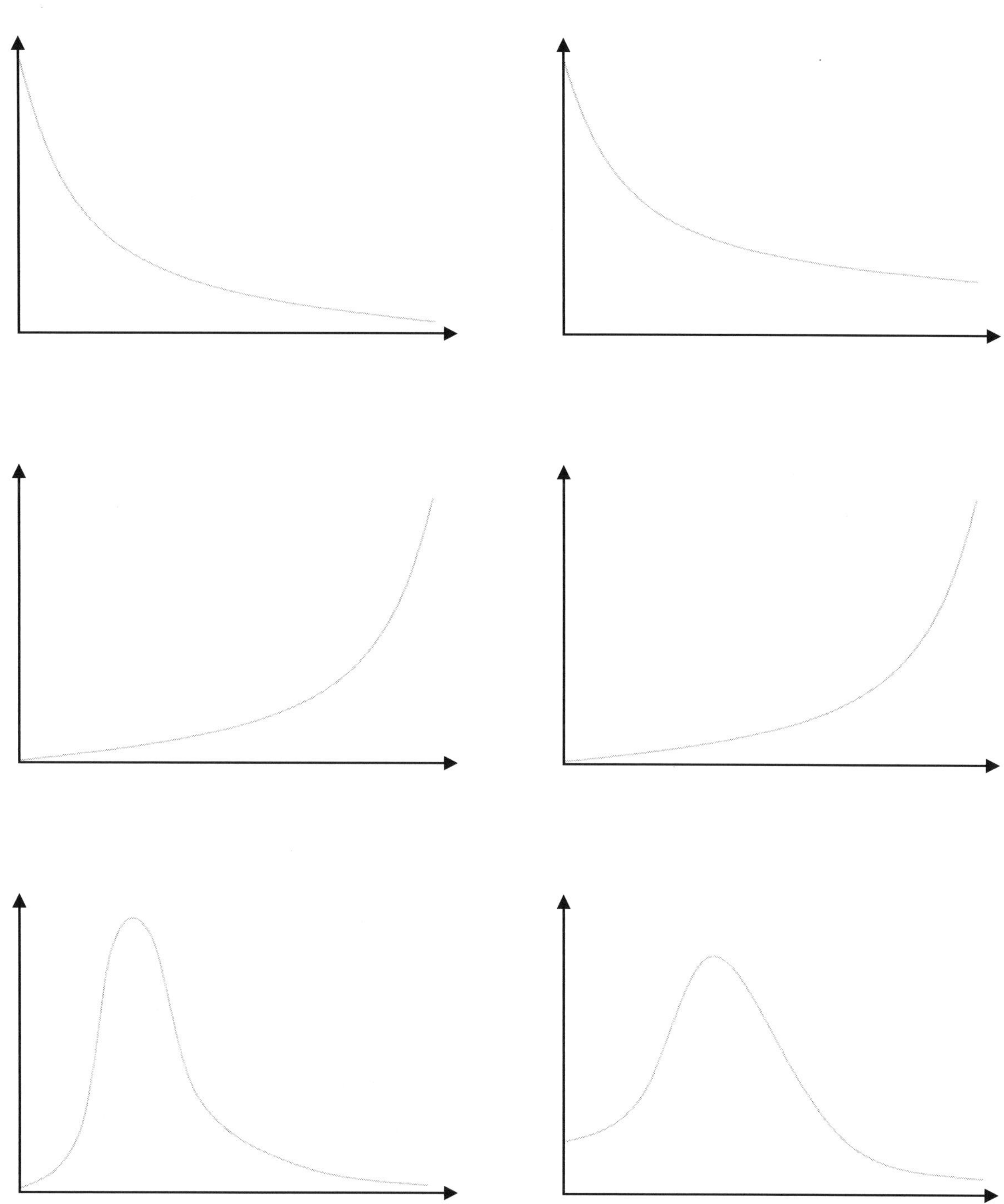

27th February

1 2 3

1. Draw the circuit symbol for a:

   a. Fixed resistor

   b. LDR

   c. Variable resistor

   d. Thermistor

   e. Diode

   f. LED

   g. Fuse

   h. Heater

   i. Voltmeter

   j. Ammeter

   k. Galvanometer

   l. Motor

   m. Loudspeaker

28th February

1

1. **Complete** the following mega table:

	Quantity	Symbol	Unit
a.	Acceleration due to gravity		
b.	Amplitude		
c.	Area		
d.	Charge		
e.	Critical angle		
f.	Current		
g.	Density		
h.	Diameter		
i.	Efficiency		
j.	Elastic potential energy		
k.	Electromotive force		
l.	Force		
m.	Frequency		
n.	Fringe spacing		
o.	Gravitational field strength		
p.	Gravitational potential energy		
q.	Height		
r.	Intensity		
s.	Internal resistance		
t.	Kinetic energy		
u.	Length		
v.	Mass		
w.	Moment		
x.	Momentum		

29th February

1. **Complete** the following mega table:

	Quantity	Symbol	Unit
a.	Period		
b.	Planck's constant		
c.	Potential difference		
d.	Power		
e.	Radius		
f.	Refractive index		
g.	Resistance		
h.	Resistivity		
i.	Slit separation		
j.	Speed		
k.	Speed of light		
l.	Spring constant		
m.	Strain		
n.	Stress		
o.	Temperature		
p.	Time		
q.	Velocity		
r.	Volume		
s.	Wave speed		
t.	Wavelength		
u.	Weight		
v.	Work done		
w.	Work function		
x.	Young modulus		

FEBRUARY REVIEW

Well done! Have a look through this workbook to see how many questions you have now completed – it's a LOT of work.

A Level Physics Content	Red	Amber	Green
I can draw common **circuit symbols**.			
I can sketch the resultant wave formed by **interfering waves**.			
I can write common quantities in their **base units**.			
I can calculate the **refractive index** of a material by measuring **angles**.			
I can recall the **symbols** and **units** of common quantities.			
I can sketch a **sinusoidal** curve.			
Any other comments:			

ANSWERS

ANSWERS

Check your work with the short answers in the back of this book.

To find full worked solutions and video support head over to:

ALevelPhysicsOnline.com/**book-2-answers**

1st November

1. 56°
2. a. volt, V

   b. ohm metre, Ω m

   c. farad, F

   d. kg m s^{-1}

   e. volt, V

   f. tesla, T
3. 1.8 J s^{-1} (W)

2nd November

1. a. 1.6 m s^{-2}

   b. About -1.1 m s^{-2}
2. 35 m

3rd November

1. a. 6.7

   b. 0.37

   c. 0.12

   d. 2.4

   e. 3.6

   f. 0.036
2. A = 1.8 mm T = 2.4 s

4th November

1. a. 10

   b. 0.099

   c. 1.2

   d. 0.11

   e. 13

   f. 1.2
2. The potential difference across a component is directly proportional to the current through it, at a constant temperature
3. A = 1.5 mm T = 4.5 ms

   f = 2.2 x 10^2 Hz

5th November

1. 62°
2. a. 2.4 %

   b. 0.25 %
3. A = 2.5 V T = 0.30 s

6th November

1. 53 cm
2. a. 1.9 %

   b. 5.4 mm

   c. 1.9 %
3. a. The distance between two adjacent points that are in phase

   b. Light that has a single wavelength (or frequency)

   c. Waves that have a constant phase difference

7th November

1. a. 85.03 3.49

   b. 16.77 1.71

   c. 8.97 1.91

   d. 3.51 0.21
2. 1.7 %
3. A = 1.8 V f = 17 Hz

8th November

1. a. 84.48 3.4

   b. 84.48 0.21

   c. 1.40 0.81

   d. 23.43 0.47
2. a. 2.4 %

   b. 2.4 %
3. t = 1.0 s (negligible air resistance

9th November

1. a. 3.6

   b. 1.2

9th November - continued

   c. 5.0

   d. 11
2. s = 39 m

10th November

1. a. 1.9

   b. 2.2

   c. 0.75

   d. 3.2
2. a. The sum of the currents entering a point in a circuit is equal to the sum of the currents leaving the same point

   b. Around any closed loop in a circuit, the sum of EMFs is equal to the sum of PDs
3. Yes

11th November

1. a. Transfers energy from one point to another.

   b. Oscillations perpendicular to the direction of energy transfer.
2. a. 1.8 %

   b. 1.8 %
3. F = 90 kN

12th November

1. X = 0.41 mm 4.9 %
2. a. 0.45 %

   b. 0.45 %
3. A = 13 V f = 3.3 Hz

13th November

1. A = 9.5 cm 2.1 %
2. v = 3.1 m s^{-1}

14th November

1. 5.8 %

14th November - continued

2.

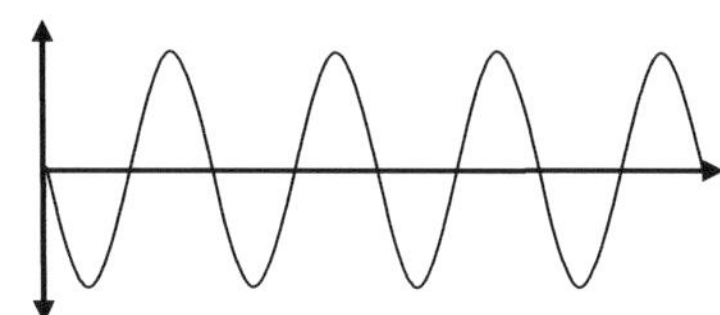

3. A = 3.8 V f = 49 Hz

15th November

1. a. ± 1 mm

   b. 31 mm

   c. ± 2 mm

   d. 6.5 %

2. Extension is directly proportional to the load, provided the elastic limit is not exceeded

16th November

1. a. ± 1 mm

   b. 29 mm

   c. ± 2 mm

   d. 6.9 %

2. a. The force exerted per unit cross sectional area

   b. The extension of an object divided by its original length

   c. The ratio of tensile stress to tensile strain.

17th November

1. a. 6.30 x 10^{-7} m

   b. 8.23 x 10^{-11} m

   c. 5.68 x 10^{-4} m^3

   d. 4.02 x 10^{16} m

   e. 13.4 m s^{-1}

2. a. 25 %

   b. 2.4 %

   c. 1.0 %

   d. The percentage uncertainty in the data reduces with repeated readings for multiple oscillations.

18th November

1. a. $M = \sqrt{M_1 M_2}$

   b. 1.52 kg

19th November

1. a. 4.9 %

   b. 4.9 %

2. a. 6.4 %

   b. 6.6 %

3. 6.3 %

20th November

1. M = 0.100 kg 3.0 %

2. 19 N 51°

3. A = 0.28 V f = 11 Hz

21st November

1. a. Material has a permanent change of shape when the load is removed

   b. Material returns to original dimensions when the load is removed

2. 3.15 x 10^7 m

22nd November

1. 7.4 %

2. $k = (4\pi^2 m) / T^2$

3. a.

   b.

   c.

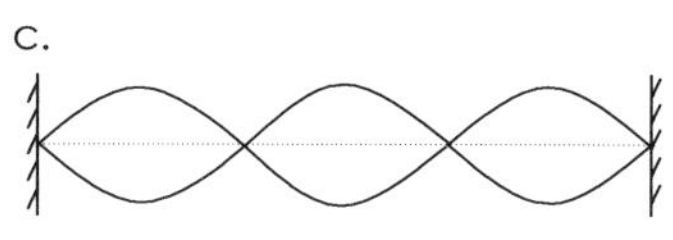

   d.

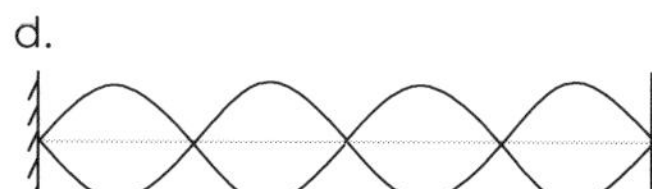

23rd November

1. 2.8 %

2. $g = (4\pi^2 l) / T^2$

3. a.

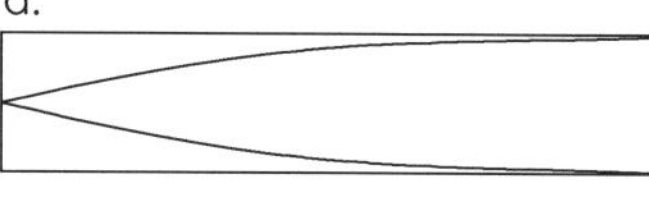

   b.

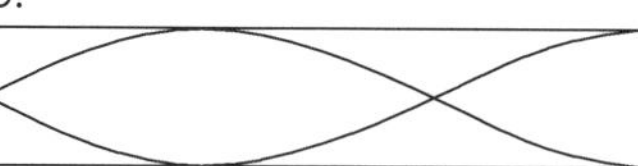

   c.

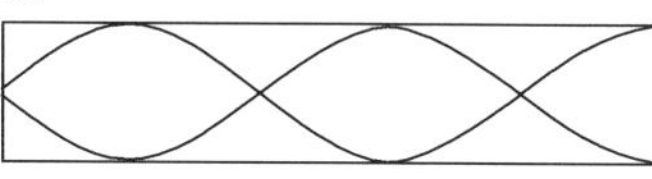

   d.

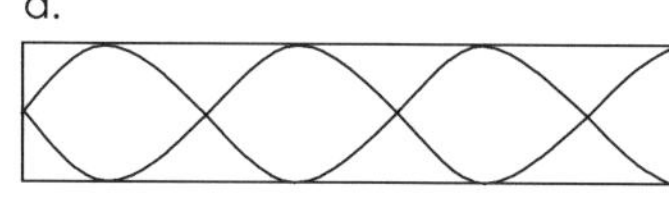

24th November

1. 5.6 %

2. a. $r = F / 6\pi\eta v$

   b. $v = F / 6\pi\eta r$

   c. $\eta = F / 6\pi r v$

3. a.

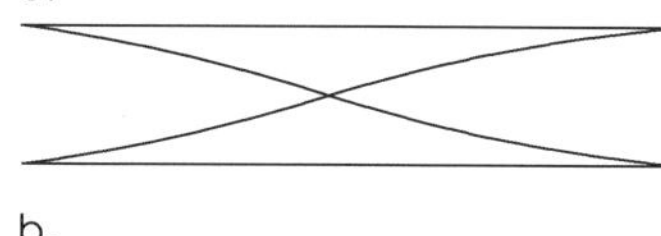

   b.

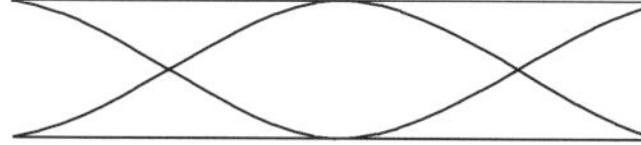

   c.

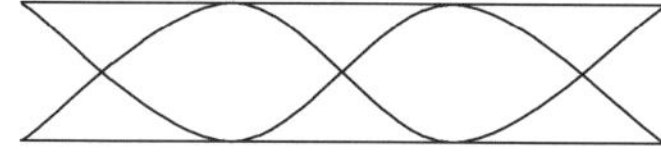

   d.

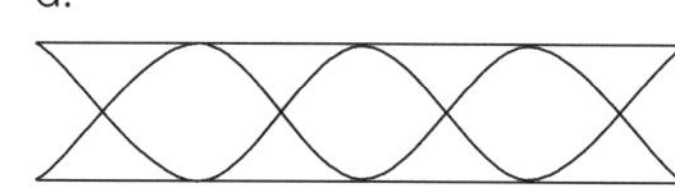

25th November

1. Straight lines of best fit

2. Lines that pass through all the error bars, can be steeper or shallower

26th November

1. $\theta_{max} = tan^{-1} (w / h)$
2. π/2 radians or 90˚

27th November

1. a. A s

   b. kg m s^{-2}

   c. kg m^2 s^{-2}

   d. kg m^2 s^{-3} A^{-1}
2. A = 1.4 V   f = 2.2 Hz

28th November

1. Lines that pass through all the error bars, can be steeper or shallower
2. Straight lines

29th November

1. a. 0.43 s

   b. 8.7 m s^{-2}

   c. t = 8.1 %   h = 0.13 %

   d. 16 %

   e. ± 1.4 m s^{-2}

30th November

1. ΣF = 0   ΣM = 0
2.
3. a.

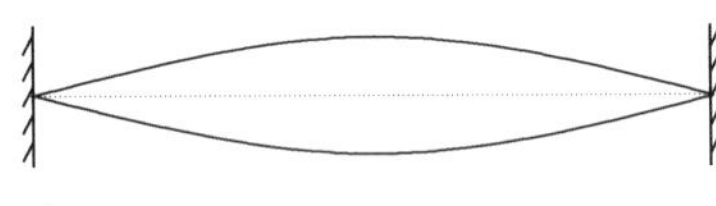

b.

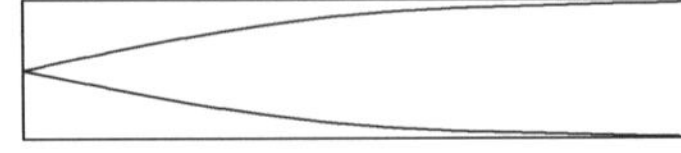

c.

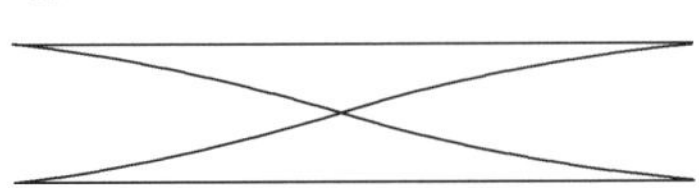

1st December

1. For a system in equilibrium:

   $\Sigma M_{Clockwise} = \Sigma M_{Anticlockwise}$
2. $p = W \cos\theta$

   $q = W \sin\theta$
3. a. 0.30 A

   b. 0.60 A

2nd December

1. Resistance is defined as the ratio of potential difference to current
2. p = 27

   q = 12
3. a. 3.4 %

   b. 6.3 or 6.4 %

3rd December

1. 9.88 ± 0.28 N kg^{-1}
2. $W_{Perpendicular}$ = 4.8 N

   $W_{Parallel}$ = 1.5 N
3. 4600 Ω

4th December

1. a. 10

   b. 2.3

   c. 2.3

   d. 7.8
2. a. About – 3.9 Ω

   b. About – 3.4 Ω

   c. About 13 %

5th December

1. a. 1.60 x 10^{-19} J

   b. 3.60 x 10^{6} J
2. Drag = 1.3 x 10^{-2} N

   NCF = 1.6 x 10^{-2} N

5th December - continued

3. a. 11 m s^{-1}

   b. 4.6 rev s^{-1}

   c. 0 m s^{-1}

   d. At the top

6th December

1. a. About – 3.4 Ω

   b. About – 3.0 Ω

   c. About 12 %
2. About 30 %

7th December

1. a. 10

   b. 3.3

   c. 6.7

   d. 8.3
2. a. 7.0 or 8.0 V

   b. From 4.1 to 9.6 %

8th December

1. a. 6.25 x 10^{18} eV

   b. 2.78 x 10^{-7} kWh
2. a. ≈ 80 kg

   b. ≈ 6 m s^{-1}

   c. ≈ 1500 kg

   d. ≈ 50 J
3. 3.3 km

9th December

1. a. 7.5 V

   b. 6.9 or 8.1 V

   c. 8.0 %
2. About 7.1 %

10th December

1. a. 4.44×10^{-26} kWh

   b. 1.04×10^{-6} J

2. a. 104 Ω

   b. ± 0.8 Ω

3. 17 m s^{-1}

11th December

1. E ≈ 6.1 V ± 8.2 %

   r ≈ 2.5 Ω

12th December

1. a. ${}^{235}_{92}U + {}^{4}_{2}He$

   b. ${}^{187}_{76}Os + {}^{0}_{-1}\beta \; (+ \bar{v}_e)$

   c. ${}^{60}_{27}Co + {}^{0}_{0}\gamma$

   d. ${}^{12}_{4}Be + {}^{1}_{0}n$

2. a = 10 b = 2.5

13th December

1.

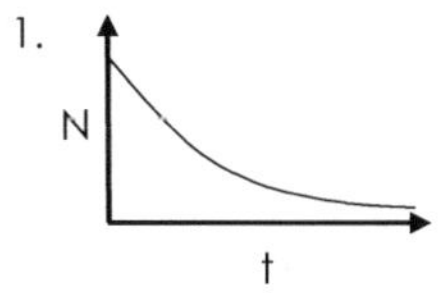

2. 1.7 ± 1.7 %

14th December

1.

N

t

2. a. a m s^{-2}

   b. C F

   c. Q C

   d. s or x m

   e. E or ε V

   f. V or V_g J kg^{-1}

14th December - continued

2. g. g N kg^{-1}

   h. I W m^{-2}

   i. φ Wb

   j. B T

   k. V V

   l. p Pa

   m. r m

   n. R Ω

   o. ρ Ω m

   p. L J kg^{-1}

   q. ε no unit

   r. σ Pa

   s. T or θ K or °C

15th December

1. 2.1 A

2. 9.58×10^{7} C kg^{-1}

3. A = 2.8 V

   f = 150 Hz

16th December

1. 2.0 V

2. 1.76×10^{11} C kg^{-1}

3. 1.0 Ω

17th December

1. ——— sine - - - - - cosine

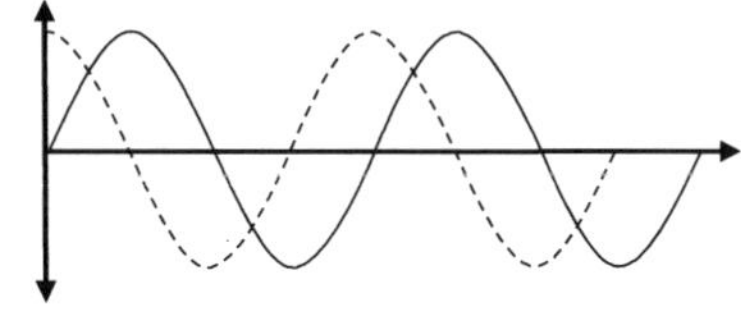

2. a. A Bq

   b. A m

   c. A m^2

   d. θ_c or c °

   e. ρ kg m^{-3}

   f. $t_{½}$ s

17th December - continued

2. g. φ Wb

   h. B T

   i. T s

   j. h J s

   k. n no unit

   l. R Ω

   m. ρ Ω m

   n. T or θ K or °C

   o. t s

   p. τ s

   q. λ m

   r. φ eV or J

   s. E Pa

18th December

1. 0 C kg^{-1}

2. 1500 kg m^{-3}

3. 4.0 V

19th December

1. 0.80 W

2. a. ω rad s^{-1}

   b. k m^2 kg s^{-2} K^{-1}

   c. F N

   d. G N m^2 kg^{-2}

   e. g N kg^{-1}

   f. V or V_g J kg^{-1}

   g. E_p J

   h. h J s

   i. n no unit

   j. c J kg^{-1} K^{-1}

   k. L J kg^{-1}

   l. c m s^{-1}

   m. k N m^{-1}

   n. ε no unit

   o. σ Pa

   p. W N

19th December - continued

2. q. W J

   r. φ eV or J

   s. E Pa

20th December

1. 17.7 m s^{-1}
2. 60 kPa
3. 1.82 kN ± 2.6 %

21st December

1. 2.6 x 10^{-3}
2. 19.6 kPa
3. 0.71 Ω

22nd December

1. a. 1.80 x 10^{-3} kg

   b. 42.6 N

23rd December

1. a. 8.49 x 10^{-2} Ω

   b. 23.0 K

24th December

1. 5.46 x 10^{-4} (1/1833)
2. The atoms of the elements consist of a number of negatively electrified corpuscles enclosed in a sphere of uniform positive electrification.

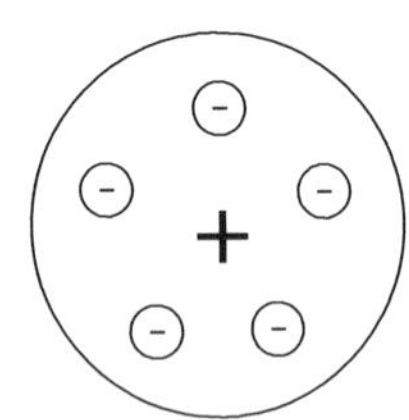

25th December

1. $^{1}_{0}n \rightarrow {}^{0}_{-1}\beta + {}^{1}_{1}p + \bar{v}_e$

25th December - continued

2. A positive central charge N e, surrounded by a compensating charge of N electrons.

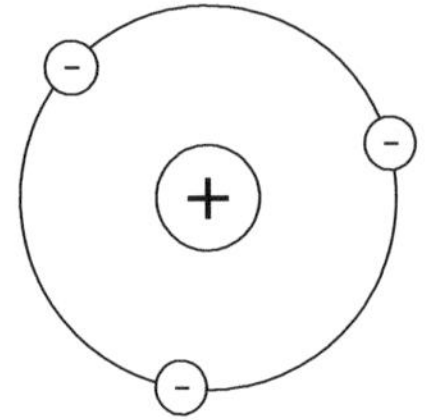

Alpha particles fired at a thin gold foil: most went through, some deflected by more than 90˚.

26th December

1. a. 3.80 X 10^{-3} m

   b. 6.42 x 10^{-3} m s^{-1}

27th December

1. a. $R_{BD} = R_3 + R_4$

   $R_{AB} = R_1 + R_3 + R_5$

   $R_{CD} = R_2 + R_4 + R_5$

   b. R_{AC} = 40 Ω

   R_{BD} = 60 Ω

   R_{AB} = 50 Ω

   R_{CD} = 100 Ω

   c. 25 Ω

28th December

1. 4.81 x 10^{7} C kg^{-1}
2. 1.08 ± 0.05 mm
3. V_N = 423 m s^{-1}

   V_E = 285 m s^{-1}

29th December

1. 125 Bq
2. V_h = 20.2 m s^{-1}

   V_v = 3.56 m s^{-1}
3. R_T = R

30th December

1. a. 9.11 x 10^{-31} kg

   b. 1.67 x 10^{-27} kg

   c. +1.60 x 10^{-19} C

   d. 1.6 x 10^{-19} J

   e. 620 – 700 nm
2. R_T = 5R/7

31st December

1. a. About 2.3 m s^{-2}

   b. About 35 m

1st January

Your answers are correct for you!

2nd January

1. a. 9.81 N kg^{-1}

   b. 6.67 x 10^{-11} N m^2 kg^{-2}

   c. 6.63 x 10^{-34} J s
2. a. The difference in angle between points on the same wave or (similar) points on two waves.

   b. The difference in the distance travelled by two waves between their source and where they meet
3.  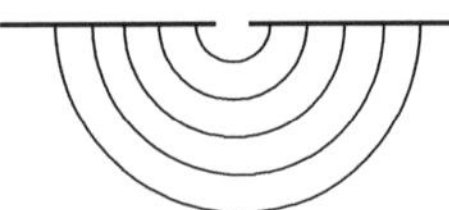

3rd January

1. a. 6.63 x 10^{-34} J s

   b. 1.38 x 10^{-23} J K^{-1}

   c. 8.31 J K^{-1} mol^{-1}
2. a. A point on a standing wave where the wave has minimum amplitude

   b. A point on a standing wave where the wave has maximum amplitude
3. 

4th January

1. 90 kJ
2. -1.99 m s^{-1}
3. 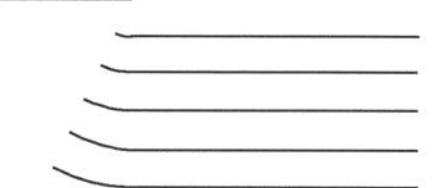

5th January

1. $\Delta\lambda = 6.25 \times 10^{-5}$ m
2. a. Energy supplied (by the cell) per unit charge

   b. Energy transferred (by a component) per unit charge
3. 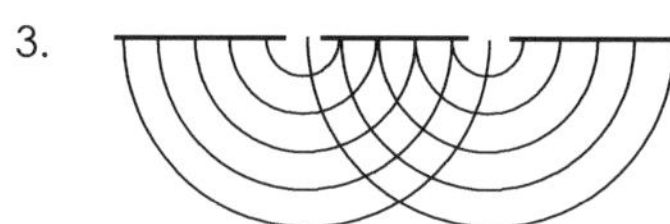

6th January

1. See the website for the full answer

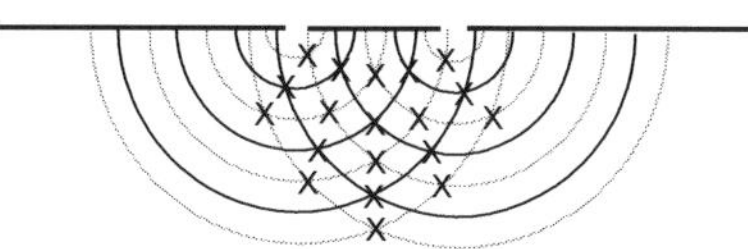

7th January

1. See the website for the full answer

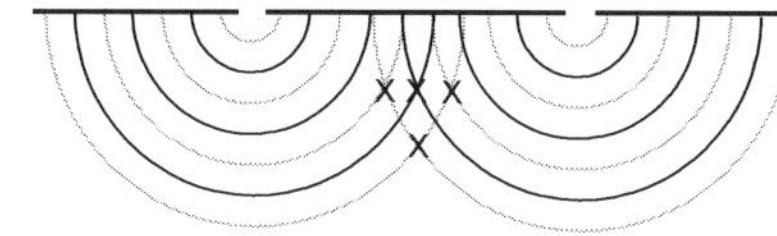

8th January

1. a. 1.60×10^{-19} C

   b. 2.90×10^{-3} m K (metre Kelvin)

   c. 1.67×10^{-27} kg
2. 0.067 m
3. a. 0.928 N m

   b. 0.928 N

9th January

1. a. 1.38×10^{-23} J K^{-1}

9th January - continued

1. b. 5.67×10^{-8} W m^{-2} K^{-4}

   c. 6.02×10^{23} mol^{-1}
2. Incoming progressive wave is reflected from end of string. This reflection has same frequency, wavelength and amplitude. Interference between these waves leads to stationary wave
3. a. 1.11 N m

   b. 2.06 N

10th January

1. a. 6.67×10^{-11} N m^2 kg^{-2}

   b. 1.38×10^{-23} J K^{-1}

   c. 8.85×10^{-12} F m^{-1}
2. 11.8 Hz
3. a. 15 N m^{-1}

   b. 0.023 J

11th January

1. 3.0 m s^{-1}
2. 18.1 m
3. a. 79 N m^{-1}

   b. 0.016 J

12th January

1. a. 6.63×10^{-34} J s

   b. 8.85×10^{-12} F m^{-1}

   c. 3.00×10^{8} m s^{-1}
2. a The ratio of potential difference across a component to the current through it

   b. The resistance within a source of EMF (due to its construction) that causes a loss of potential difference when current flows
3. a. 5.24 N

   b. 7.55 N

13th January

1. 61°
2. 6.0 %
3. 1.54×10^{-4} kg m^{-1}

14th January

1. a. 0.0624, 0.125, 0.249, 0.500, 1.00

   b. A lovely straight line

   c. 1.41

   d. $\sqrt{2}$

   e. 0.707 m

15th January

1. 40°
2.

a. A	m^2
b. B	T
c. C	F
d. d	m
e. E or ε	V
f. F	N
g. G	N m^2 kg^{-2}
h. h	J s
i. I	A
j. j	m s^{-3}
k. k	J K^{-1}
l. L	m
m. m	kg
n. n	no unit
o. σ	Pa
p. p	kg m s^{-1}
q. Q	C
r. r	m
s. s	m

16th January

1. a. 1.27×10^{-4} m^2

   b. 2.03×10^{-7} m^2

16th January - continued

1. c. 7.79×10^{-8} m^2

   d. 4.9×10^{-10} m^2

2. 1.52 13.04

3. 2.0

17th January

1. 30°

2. 1.21 13.54

3. 3.0 N s

18th January

1. 1.24×10^4 N

2. 1.26 11.57

3. 160 N s

19th January

1. a. $M = -rV_g / G$

   b. $M = -gr^2 / G$

   c. $M = -Fr^2 / Gm$

2. 1.54 14.25

3. About 175 N s

20th January

1. a. 1.00×10^{-5} m^3

   b. 1.0×10^{-3} m^3

   c. 3.3×10^{-4} m^3

   d. 5.00×10^{-4} m^3

2. 96 m

3. Quiet sound due to path difference = λ/2 therefore destructive interference

21st January

1. a. 6.63×10^{-34} J s

   b. 1.38×10^{-23} J K^{-1}

   c. 8.31 J mol^{-1} K^{-1}

2. 3.8×10^{-3} m

3. About 67 m s^{-1}

22nd January

1.

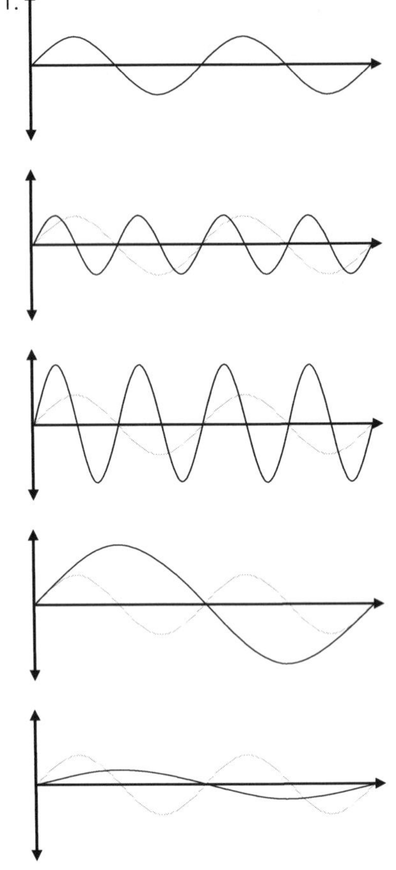

23rd January

1. 1.0×10^9

2. 7

3. 36 m

24th January

1. a. 6.67×10^{-11} N m^2 kg^{-2}

   b. 5.67×10^{-8} W m^{-2} K^{-4}

   c. 1.661×10^{-27} kg

2. 7.51 59.41

3. 2.0 m

25th January

1. Any three from: travel at the same speed (3.00×10^8 m s^{-1}) in a vacuum, transfer energy, involve oscillations in the electric and magnetic fields, involve oscillations that are perpendicular to the direction of travel (transverse)

25th January - continued

2. 5.92×10^8 Pa

3. About 16.5 m

26th January

1.

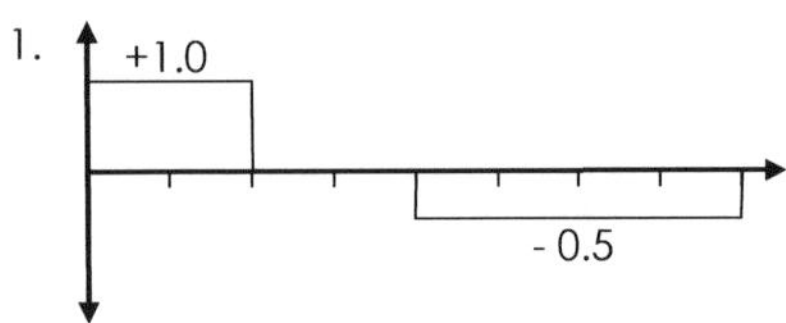

2.

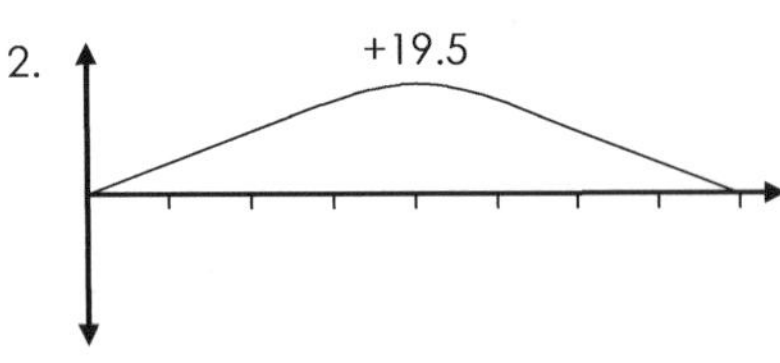

27th January

1.

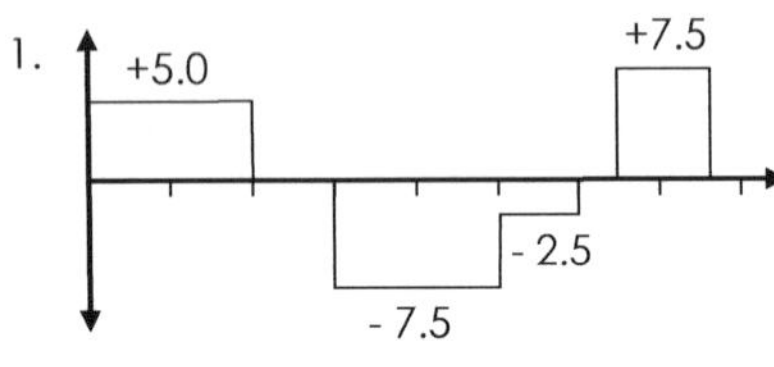

2.

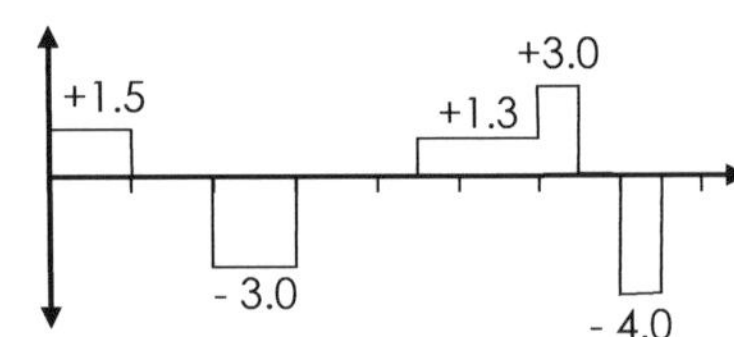

28th January

1. 0.072 m

2. a. A wave that transfers energy

   b. A wave on which there are points that are nodes and antinodes

3 Silver

29th January

1. a. 1.4×10^{19} Hz

   b. 2.82×10^{14} Hz

   c. About 4.3×10^{14} Hz

29th January - continued

2. α $m = 6.64 \times 10^{-27}$ kg

 $Q = +3.20 \times 10^{-19}$ C

 Low

 β $m = 9.11 \times 10^{-31}$ kg

 $Q = -1.60 \times 10^{-19}$ C

 Medium

 γ $m = 0$

 $Q = 0$

 High

3. 3.3 N

30th January

1. a. 6.63×10^{-34} J s

 b. 1.38×10^{-23} J K^{-1}

 c. 8.31J mol^{-1} K^{-1}

2. 1.3

3. 0.086 m s^{-1}

31st January

1. a. kg m s^{-1}

 b. Ω m

 c. J or eV

 d. N s

2. 29 m

1st February

1. 13 cm

2. 90 C

3. a. 1.3 m

 b. 0.65 m

 c. 0.43 m

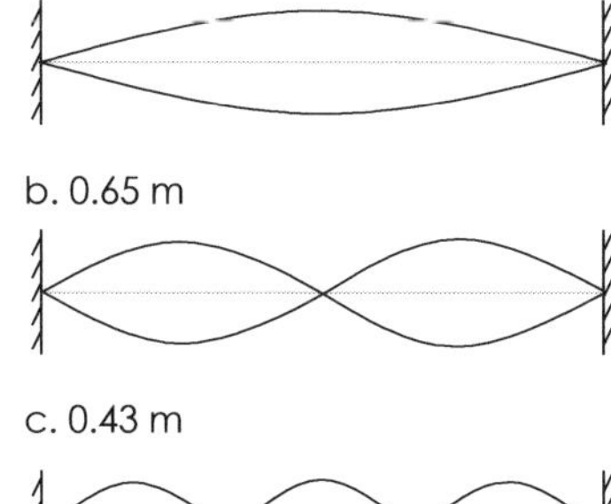

2nd February

1. 0.026 A

2. a. $\Sigma I_{in} = \Sigma I_{out}$

 b. ΣE = ΣV

3. a. 3.2 m

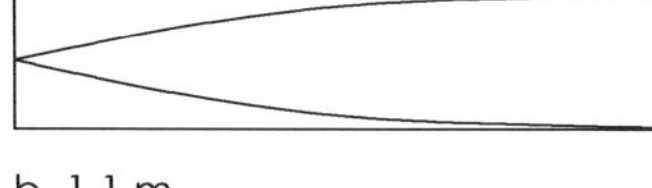

 b. 1.1 m

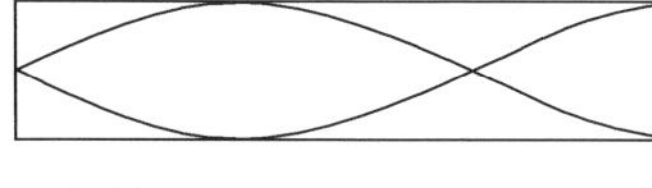

 c. 0.64 m

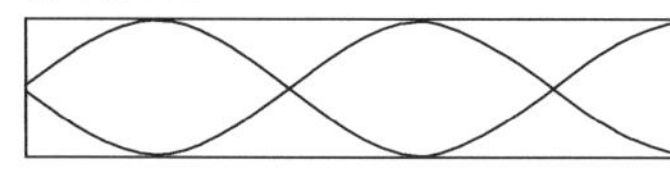

3rd February

1. a. 40 kN m

 b. 28.3 kN m

 c. cosine curve

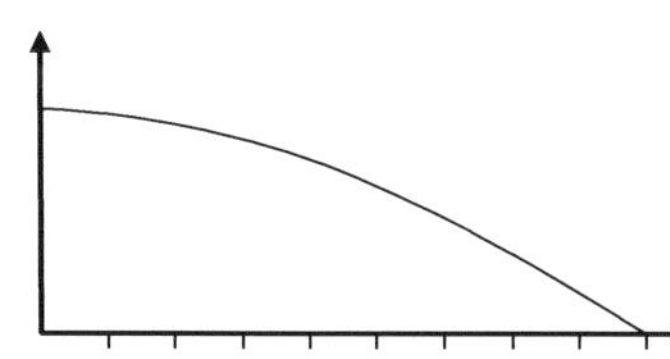

4th February

1. a. 9.11×10^{-31} kg

 b. 6.02×10^{23} mol^{-1}

 c. 2.90×10^{-3} m k

2. a. $h = E / f$

 b. i. 6.63×10^{-34} J s

 ii. 1.62×10^{-35} m

 iii. 5.39×10^{-44} s

3. a. Superconductors have zero resistance below a critical temperature.

 b. Used in MRI machines and particle colliders as they can handle very large currents and therefore can produce very strong magnetic fields.

 c. High-temperature superconductors are still below room temperature but are much cheaper to run as they do not have to be as cold.

5th February

1. 0.25 Ω

2.

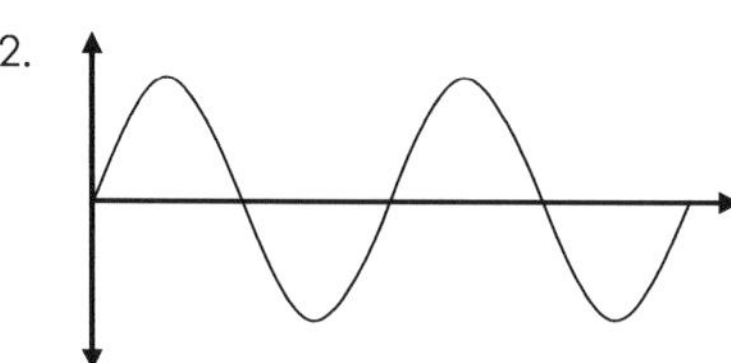

6th February

1. 6 in total

 Up, Charm, Top + 2/3

 Down, Strange, Bottom – 1/3

2.

7th February

1. a. 630 nm

 b. 1.32 GW

 c. 40.2 TJ

 d. 42.0 ms

2. a. Momentum and kinetic energy conserved

 b. Momentum conserved but the maximum loss of kinetic energy – the two bodies move off together

3. 0.52 Ω

8th February

1. a. 1.02×10^{-2} m

 b. 8.4×10^{-8} m

 c. 2.03×10^{8} eV

 d. 7.97×10^{5} pc

2.

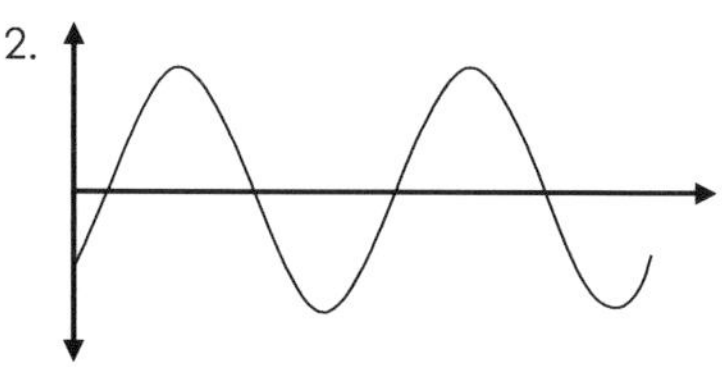

9th February

1. The energy due to the mass of the particle. The famous equation $E = mc^2$ is useful for converting the mass into energy in joules. Note: kinetic energy is not part of this energy, to work out the total energy you sum the rest and kinetic energies

2. Laser, stand, diffraction grating, metre ruler, 30 cm ruler

   Shine on a non-reflective to reduce any specular reflection - don't look directly into the laser

3. 63 %

10th February

1. $F_V = 3.4$ N

   $F_H = 7.3$ N

2. 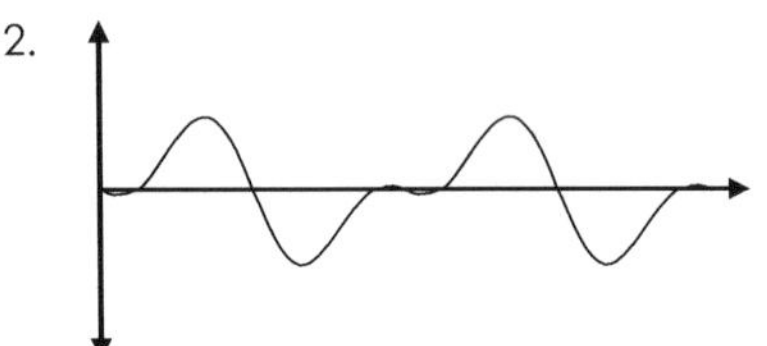

11th February

1. $v_N = 14$ m s^{-1}

   $v_E = 25$ m s^{-1}

2. 4.21 32.85

3. a. 5.0 5.9 1.18

   b. 23 4.1 0.18

   c. 1.9 1.9 1.0

   d. 2.2 2.2 1.0

12th February

1. Acceleration, upthrust and momentum

2. 0.050 m

3. a. 5.0 3.7 0.74

   b. 3.0 2.2 0.74

   c. 41 4.1 0.10

   d. 41 4.1 0.10

   e. 1.9 1.0 0.54

   f. 5.7 3.1 0.54

13th February

1. Time period, potential difference, pressure, density and work done

2. 1.5×10^{20} electrons

3. 15 %

14th February

1. 7.0 kN

2. 7.4 %

3. a. 0.89 0.040

   b. 1.9 0.040

   c. 0.21 0.012

   d. 0.21 0.0071

   e. 0.21 0.021

15th February

1. a. 1.3×10^{-5} m^2

   b. 1.3×10^{-3} m^2

   c. 13 m^2

2. 0.83 W m^{-2}

3. About 80 m s^{-2}

16th February

1. 3.16×10^{-19} J

2. 15 Ω

3. 1.4 (r = 34°)

17th February

1. 7.2 J

2. About 47 m (negligible air resistance)

3. 3.2 to 5.6 V

18th February

1. 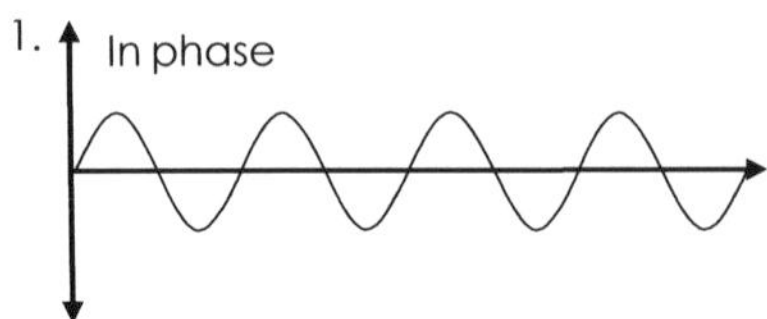

18th February - continued

1. 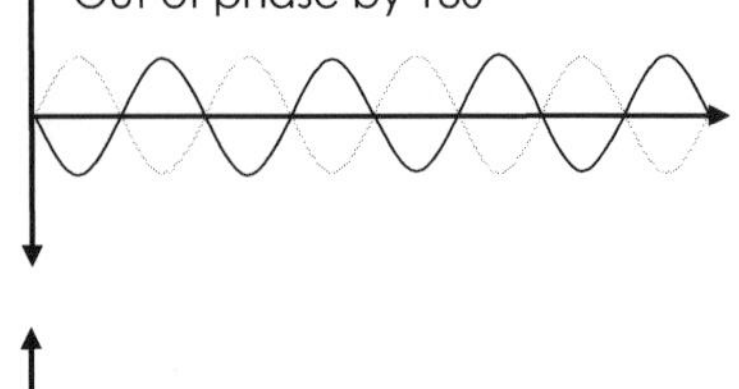

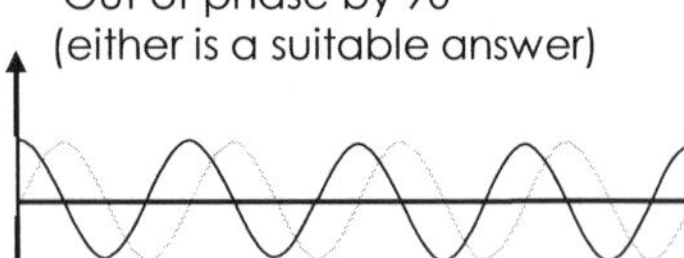

Out of phase by 90°
(either is a suitable answer)

19th February

1. 225 J

2. 0.10 J

3. A ≈ 0.62 V f = 3.3 Hz

20th February

1. 27.8 g ± 2.7 %

2. 539 m

3. a. 3.00×10^3 eV

   b. 4.8×10^{-16} J

   c. 3.25×10^7 m s^{-1}

21st February

1. a. 3.2×10^{-19} J

   b. 3.6×10^{-19} J

   c. 4.4×10^{-19} J

2. 70.9°

3. Max of 10.2 m at 45°

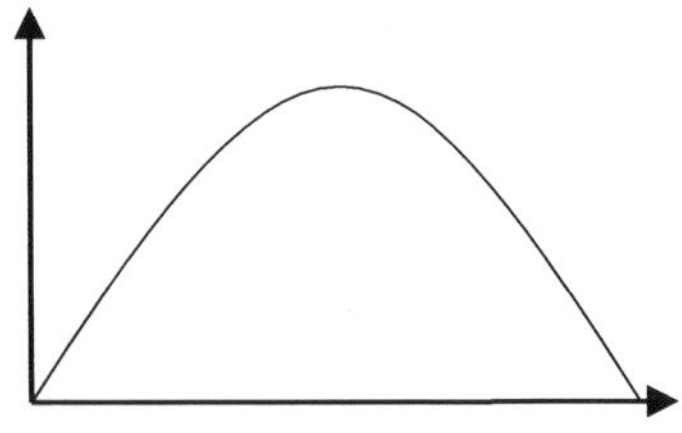

22nd February

1. 72 kN
2.

a. kg	kg
b. m	m
c. s	s
d. m s^{-1}	m s^{-1}
e. m s^{-2}	m s^{-2}
f. kg m s^{-1}	kg m s^{-1}
g. N s	kg m s^{-1}
h. N	kg m s^{-2}
i. J	kg m^2 s^{-2}
j. A	A
k. C	A s
l. V	kg m^2 s^{-3} A^{-1}
m. Ω	kg m^2 s^{-3} A^{-2}
n. K	K
o. J kg^{-1} K^{-1}	m^2 s^{-2} K^{-1}

23rd February

1. a. 0.0449, 0.0655, 0.0841, 0.106, 0.232*, 0.145

   b. Points plotted and a straight line of best fit – *ignore anomaly

   c. About 10 m s^{-2}

   d. Time lag due to residual magnetic field before ball falls etc

24th February

1. a. ≈ 6 ms^{-1}

   b. ≈ 2000 kg

   c. ≈ 880 N
2. 2.7 x 10^{-11} m
3.

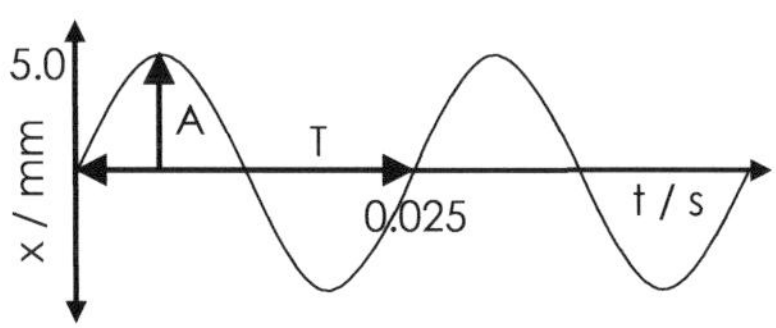

25th February

1. 2.2 A
2. 4.80 m   67 Hz (if 330 m s^{-1} used)
3. 29 m s^{-1} at 31° from vertical

26th February

1. Perfect smooth lines
2. Perfect smooth lines (even better than Book 1)

27th February

1. a.

   b. 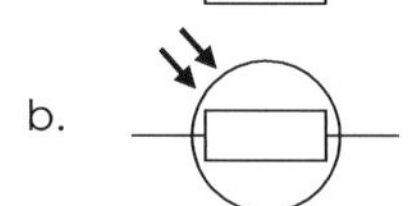

   c.

   d.

   e.

   f.

   g.

   h.

   i. V

   j. A

   k. G

   l. M

   m.

28th February

1.

a. g	m s^{-2}
b. A	m
c. A	m^2
d. Q	C
e. C or θ_c	°
f. I	A
g. ρ	kg m^{-3}
h. d	m
i. η	no units
j. E_e	J
k. E or ε	V
l. F	N
m. f	Hz
n. w or x	m
o. g	N kg^{-1}
p. E_p	J
q. h	m
r. I	W m^{-2}
s. r	Ω
t. E_k	J
u. L	m
v. m	kg
w. M	N m
x. p	kg m s^{-1}

29th February

1.

a. T	s
b. h	J s
c. V	V
d. P	W
e. r	m
f. n	no units
g. R	Ω
h. ρ	Ω m
i. a or s	m
j. v	m s^{-1}
k. c	m s^{-1}

29th February - continued

1. l. k N m^{-1}

l. k	N m^{-1}
m. ε	no units
n. σ	Pa
o. T or θ	K or °C
p. t	s
q. v	m s^{-1}
r. V	m^3
s. v or c	m s^{-1}
t. λ	m
u. W	N
v. W	J
w. φ	J or eV
x. E	Pa

PHYSICS ONLINE

LEWIS MATHESON

A former **Physics Teacher** and Head of Science, I began making videos to support students back in 2015. Now, I have established websites specialising in GCSE and A Level Physics as well as thousands of subscribers and followers on YouTube and TikTok.

Furthermore, I continue to work with many organisations to support teachers, including the Royal Academy of Engineering, Ogden Trust, Institute of Physics, and STEM Learning.

WEBSITES AND SCHOOL SUBSCRIPTIONS

Hundreds of schools now have full access to dedicated websites for both **GCSE** and **A Level Physics** – every day thousands of students access high-quality videos whenever they need them; these videos include practical experiments, livestreams, worked examples, and regular updates about exams.

Have a look at **ALevelPhysicsOnline.com** to find out more about a **Premium Plan** or **School Subscription** to the website.

Printed in Great Britain
by Amazon